ETHICS

The Science of Oughtness

ABBREVIATED EDITION

ISBN: 0–911714–15–4   LC No.: 84–52234

Archie J. Bahm
Albuquerque, New

ETHICS

The Science of Oughtness

ABBREVIATED EDITION

Archie J. Bahm
Professor of Philosophy Emeritus
University of New Mexico

Albuquerque

1984

Copyright by Archie J. Bahm, 1980
Abbreviated Edition, 1984

Quotations up to three pages or equivalent permitted without special permission provided source of quotation
is appropriately noted.

WORLD BOOKS
Published by Archie J. Bahm, Publisher
1915 Las Lomas Road N.E.
Albuquerque, New Mexico 87106
U.S.A.

ISBN: 0-911714-12-X (1980)
ISBN: 0-911714-15-4 1984

LC No: 84-52234

Printed in U.S.A.

CONTENTS

BOOKS BY THE AUTHOR

WHY BE MORAL? AN INTRODUCTION TO ETHICS, 1980
ETHICS AS A BEHAVIORAL SCIENCE, 1974
WHAT MAKES ACTS RIGHT? 1958
PHILOSOPHY: AN INTRODUCTION, 1953, 1964
METAPHYSICS: AN INTRODUCTION, 1974
THE WORLD'S LIVING RELIGIONS, 1964, 1971, 1977
COMPARATIVE PHILOSOPHY, 1977, 1978
THE PHILOSOPHER'S WORLD MODEL, 1979
INTERDEPENDENCE, Ed., 1977
POLARITY, DIALECTIC, AND ORGANICITY, 1970, 1977
PHILOSOPHY OF THE BUDDHA, 1958, 1962, 1969
BHAGAVAD GITA: THE WISDOM OF KRISHNA, 1970
YOGA: UNION WITH THE ULTIMATE, 1961, 1978
YOGA FOR BUSINESS EXECUTIVES, 1965, 1967, 1970
TAO TEH KING by LAO TZU, 1958
THE HEART OF CONFUCIUS, 1969, 1971, 1977
LOGIC FOR BEGINNERS, 1960

Chapter II

THE NATURE OF OUGHTNESS

THE NATURE OF OUGHTNESS

WHAT IS ETHICS?

Ethics includes both theory and practice.
Concern for ethical practices will not detain
us here. The present volume pertains to theory,
to inquiry into the nature of ethics. Some
inquiries are casual, some describe types of
behavior, and some focus on ethical problems.
The present inquiry aims to show that scientific methods can be used to inquire into the
nature of ethics and its problems and that reliable conclusions useful for guiding ethical
practices can be obtained.

I propose as an hypothesis about the nature
of ethics as a field of scientific inquiry that
its most basic problem, one that is involved
in all other ethical problems, is "What is the
nature of oughtness?" In this sense, ethics
is the science of oughtness.

Closely related is inquiry into the nature
of rightness and wrongness. Ethics is concerned with obligation and duty, but since these
terms are almost synonyms for oughtness, they
will not require separate treatment here. Some
investigators focus on codes, standards or
norms for conduct, some on mores, laws and institutions, some on the language used in moral
discourse. All of these are problems for scientific inquiry, but they appear to be secondary and derivative from the more basic problems of the nature of oughtness and rightness.
Questions about the nature of conscience, justice and rights must be included in our investigation and, although clues for answering
them can be found already in the nature of
oughtness and rightness, one does not fully
understand the nature of oughtness until he
understands how it occurs as an oughtness of

justice and an oughtness of rights and manifests itself in feelings of conscience.

Some investigators mistakenly assume that
ethics is merely social and others that it is
merely personal. I will show why ethics pertains to something that is essentially personal
and also essentially social and why most of
what is personal and what is social involves
the other interdependently. I shall propose
as essential to ethics some principles for
choosing, and some principles for choosing for
a group. Some of these principles will seem
self-evident. All of them can be tested by
rigorous examination. All of them presuppose
that persons involve values, intrinsic values,
and that at least some of these values can be
known and considered in making right and wrong
choices. Fully adequate understanding of the
nature of oughtness and rightness involves understanding the nature of values.

WHAT IS OUGHTNESS?

Oughtness consists in the power that an apparently greater good has over an apparently
lesser good, or an apparently lesser evil[1] has
over an apparently greater evil, or an apparent
good has over an apparent evil, in compelling
our choices.[2]

In one very fundamental sense, this statement is a complete account of the nature of
ethics. Nothing more need be said. For it
states something universal as involved in everything that can properly be called ethical. It
is a basis for everything else in ethics. Whenever oughtness is missing, ethics is absent.
A complete account of the nature and conditions
and kinds of oughtness would be a complete account of ethics.

However, there is much more to ethics, because there are many conditions, essential and

36

occasional, of the existence of oughtness,
there are many different kinds of oughtness,
and there are many uncertainties regarding the
conditions and kinds, both apparent and real,
that call for inquiry and understanding. Since
oughtness exists whenever choices occur, and
since most of waking time is occupied with
choosing, oughtness comes close to being both
omnipresent and omnicomplicated, i.e., as complicated as choices can become. So, in another
important sense, a complete account of ethics
is impossible. As long as new kinds of choices
occur to mankind, a complete account of ethics
will always be impossible.

1. Why greater good? Why ought one choose
a greater good in preference to a lesser good?
Precisely because it is a good and greater. Why
ought one choose a lesser evil in preference to
a greater evil? Precisely because it is an evil
and lesser. Why ought one choose a good in
preference to a bad? Precisely because it is
a good and not a bad. The ultimate bases for
oughtness of choices are the intrinsic goods
and bads apparently involved.

Goods and bads are of two kinds: intrinsic,
or ends-in-themselves, and instrumental, or
means-to-ends. Intrinsic goods are good-in-
themselves. Intrinsic evils are bad-in-them-
selves. Whatever is instrumental in causing
or maintaining or consummating an intrinsic
good is thereby is an instrumental good or has
instrumental goodness. Whatever is instrumental in causing or maintaining or consumating an
intrinsic bad thereby is an instrumental bad
or has instrumental badness.

Some things are both good and bad. Some experiences involve both intrinsic goods and intrinsic evils, both enjoyments and sufferings.
Some things may cause intrinsic goods at some
times and intrinsic bads at other times, or
even at the same time. Some things are both

instrumentally good and instrumentally bad at
the same time.

Some things have been intrinsic goodness and
instrumental goodness at the same time. Enjoyment at one time may be instrumental in causing
enjoyment at another time. The first enjoyment
is intrinsic value and its causing later enjoyment constitutes it as having instrumental value. Some things have both intrinsic badness
and instrumental badness at the same time. A
pain may cause me to jerk my hand and bump it
causing another pain. The first pain is an intrinsic evil and its causing the second pain
constitutes it as having instrumental evil.
Some things have both intrinsic goodness and
instrumental evil. Enjoying excitement may lead
to vigorous action resulting in pain. Some
things have both intrinsic evil and instrumental goodness. Suffering a pain in my tooth may
lead to dental extraction and enjoyment of
painless eating.

The point of including the above remarks
here is to remind us of how numerous, complex,
and intermingled are the factors in apparent
values in addition to those factors constituting
the objects about which choices are being made.
These complications cannot be reviewed here.
See Axiology: The Science of Values, especially Chapter III, "Nature of Values," for details.

Sometimes awareness is occupied by a choice
between two intrinsic values: "Do I prefer warm
or warmer?" Sometimes awareness is occupied by
a choice between two instrumental values: "Will
a pen or a pencil be more useful?" Many choices,
perhaps most choices made by highly-educated
professionally-trained adults, involve complexes of intrinsic and instrumental values gestal-
tified in dynamic configurations from which it
is difficult to analyse the many different kinds
of values intermingling in them. But all are
ethical, or involve oughtness, whenever, or to

the extent that, they involve choices between apparently greater and lesser goods and bads.

2. Why apparent good? Although the ultimate bases of oughtness are intrinsic values, their availability for evaluative judgment involved in choosing consists in the way they appear to a judger at the time of choosing. What does not appear to the judger at the time of his choosing does not receive recognition as relevant to the choice and so does not participate in constituting an actual ought.[3]

Since people do make mistakes, appearances, all of which appear as true, may involve inadequacies and falsities. One who discovers that some appearances are false usually desires to improve their veridity. The problem of how to eliminate false appearances and to minimize false judgments is another problem, one of the most important problems in ethical theory and practice. It exists as an ethical problem for each person discovering such falsity and having hope for removing it. It exists as an ethical problem for each group concerned about the reliability of member judgments. But on each occasion for choosing, what one ought to choose will depend on present appearances.

The problem of understanding the nature of error and falsity is one of those constituting epistemology, the science of knowing. The problem of learning more and more about the nature of things so that errors of judgment of appearances may be reduced is one constituting the science of education. Ethics as a science depends on these other sciences for research needed for understanding the knowing and learning factors influencing ethical decisions. Ethics as a science has vested interests in improvements in these fields and in all other sciences producing conclusions useful for increasing the adequacy and truthfulness of appearances, including apparent

values, as a way of improving the quality of
feelings of oughtness based on them.

In absence of assurance that what appears
is also real, one must still choose in terms
of what appears. Uncertainty about appearances
functions as uncertainty about how one ought to
choose. Thus some oughts exist as more uncertain than others.[4] This problem will be recon-
sidered below when the role and nature of intentions are examined. Sometimes the alternatives chosen seem very obvious and the obligation to choose very compulsive. At other times
the differences between the alternatives seem
so small that the choice is experienced more as
weak consent than as a compulsion. Thus oughts
vary widely in their compulsiveness. Some persons seem to have dogmatic temperaments and experience their oughts as very compulsive. Others
have considerable timidity and experience their
oughts with considerable tentativity. But for
each, oughtness is experienced in terms of how
the goods and bads appear at a time of choosing.

Apparent value is an ultimate constituent in
oughtness. Although the intrinsic values are
the ultimate bases for all actual oughts, only
those values that appear at the time of choosing
are considered in such choosing. The oughtness
with which ethics as a science is concerned depends ultimately on such appearances.

3. Why compelling? Whenever an appearance
appears, apprehension of it involves an attitude of accepting it. Although such acceptance
is usually spontaneous and transparent (i.e.,
does not call attention to itself), it involves
some degree of judgment that what appears appears. When one good appears as greater than
another, whatever compusion a person feels to
assert that what appears appears functions as
a compulsion to assert that the one good appears as greater than the other. That asser-
tion functions as a choice. So whatever com-

pulsion one feels to assert that one good appears as greater than another functions also as a feeling of compulsion to choose the apparently greater good. Any obviousness of the apparent difference in value has a feeling of compulsion about it. One intuits his feeling of compulsion just as directly as he intuits his feelings of enjoyment and suffering and just as directly as he intuits the apparent differences between two enjoyments.

In what does the power of such compulsion consist? Disregarding all of the causes of the existence of each occasion for choosing,[5] I locate the apparent power felt as compulsion to choose in the willingness to accept, to assent to, or to assert that, one value, and ultimately some intrinsic value, appears to be the greater (i.e., involves more intrinsic value) than the other. Although one can easily make too much of teleological causation, here the apparently greater good (being or involving greater intrinsic good) is the ultimate locus of whatever power is attributed to the feeling of compulsion to choose it. So far as the nature of oughtness is concerned, one needs to look no further.

Thus far I have considered only compulsion to choose, not compulsion to act. A person may choose between to alternatives, deciding that one is better than another, without further action. The issue of whether or not to act may involve another choice between apparent alternatives regarding which appears better. If acting appears better, then the feeling of compulsion to choose this alternative functions also as a feeling of compulsion to act.

In fact, ordinary behavior normally includes a continuing series of choices both about which of two or more alternatives is better and about whether or not to act on the better alternative is better. Ethical conduct is not, as some

seem to think, simple conformity to some moral
rule; actually it consists in perpetual confron-
tation with a series of choices each one of
which must be decided on its own terms, i.e, in
terms of the way the alternatives appear. Something so common as the feeling of compulsion to
choose the better surely is something with which
everyone is well acquainted.[6]

4. Actual and conditional oughtness. Discussion thus far has dealt primarily with actual
oughtness, the feeling of obligation compelling
one to choose between the better of two or more
alternatives at a particular time. But much if
not most discussions about ethics pertain to how
one ought to choose and act in kinds of situations one is not now confronting. "If another
car is tailgating you, then what ought you to
do?" Such discussion pertains not to a present
situation with a present ought but to a possible
situation that may exist and that will exist
if and when all of the necessary conditions cooperate. Any ought that may be asserted relative to such a situation is here called "a
conditional ought."

Each actual ought that exists as a feeling
of compulsion to choose is a product of many
causal conditions. While one is feeling such
compulsion, he may not be aware of all, or even
any, of the conditions causing him to choose.
Sometimes we feel obligated to choose without
knowing why. But many times we do know some of
the causes of our choosing situation. We may
have prepared for it deliberately, as when
serving two deserts at a party where each guest
must choose between them. Some actual oughts
occur when a person is aware of complexes of
causes each of which has a significant contribution to make to the numerous values at stake
in making a choice. When this is so, and at
the moment of choice one is unsure of the relative importance of each value factor, one

chooses with some uncertainty, even though
with some finality when a course cannot be
reversed. Sometimes actual oughts occur suddenly, as when a child darts in front of your
speeding car. Time does not permit examining
alternatives since spontaneous reaction is
needed.

The significance of considering conditional
oughts is that many of these can be examined
before they become contributing factors in
future actual oughts and may be examined in
sufficient detail so that decisions about
their relative importance can be made in ad-
vance. If one learns, on the basis of experience or from research by others, that speeding
cars on crowded streets are more likely to
cause child deaths, then he may later recall
this probability and reduce his speed on a
particular occasion. Recalling the principle
then contributes to an actual feeling of oughtness to reduce speed. But becoming aware of
the principle when one is not driving may give
one a conditional feeling of obligation: "Whenever I drive on a crowded street, I ought to
reduce my speed." Here is an ought about a
condition not now existing. I am not now driving on a crowded street, so I do not now have
an actual ought to reduce speed. Here we have
an example of a conditional ought and one
clearly recognized as such.

Driver-training programs, which are among
the most effective ethical instruction and
learning programs in the United States, sometimes include principles that some drivers
never find use for and thus never become actualized in their lives. Rural drivers often
swing to the left side of a road when making
a right turn. City drivers who never drive
on rural roads may never have occasions for
such a conditional ought to fuction actually.
Yet a thorough driver-training program should

warn potential drivers: "When driving on a
rural road, be sure that a person moving to
the left side of a road is not intending to
make a right turn before passing him."

One thing to notice about conditional oughts
is that we become aware of many that never become actualized in our lives. Thus we may
realize that ethical thinking, including ethics
as a science, is often occupied by, and intense-
ly concerned about, conditional oughts much more
than actual oughts. Conditional oughts have
their reason for being in actual oughts. But
actual oughts are of so many kinds and vary
so much in complexities that the numbers and
kinds of conditional oughts seem to occur in
endless varieties.

The distinction between actual and conditional oughts is essential to clear understanding of the nature of ethics. Like the distinction in axiology between intrinsic and instrumental values,[7] it should be kept in mind at
all times or should so condition habituated
thinking that it is recalled spontaneously
whenever dangers from confusion occur. The
distinction is of sufficient importance that
the two kinds of oughtness are treated in
separate sections following.

ACTUAL OUGHTNESS

Although most feelings of actual oughtness
occur **unanalyzed** and although some persons seem
to believe that such feelings cannot be analyzed,
much inquiry into the nature of actual oughtness
has occurred. Without reviewing the long history of such inquiry, I present as an hypothesis,
or as a collection of hypotheses, the following
statements about what appear to me to be essential conditions of the existence of actual
oughts.[8]

1. Essential conditions of oughtness.

a. All actual oughts are experienced, or depend on awareness or consciousness, for their actual existence.

b. All involve values, as discussed in Axiology: The Science of Values, Chapter III, including intrinsic and instrumental values, potential and actual values, and experiencing values as objects.

c. All involve choices between alternatives.

d. All involve volition or intention.[9]

e. All involve feelings, for all actual oughts or obligations are, or involve, feelings of oughtness or obligation.

f. All are intuited or apprehended directly because all feelings are intuited or apprehended directly.

g. All are subjective in the sense that they are, or involve, feelings. Furthermore, all are subjective in the sense that all of the ideas in terms of which obligations are conceived also occur in consciousness.

h. All involve conceptualization. Although there may be times when one feels that he ought to do something without knowing quite what it is that he ought to do, he can hardly feel that he has obligation in the full sense until he begins to become clear about what he ought to do. That is, one may believe that he has obligations about which he is unclear, but may also feel uncertain about what his obligations are and how much he is obligated so long as lack of clarity in conception and lack of assurance regarding his understanding of the issues at stake remain. Hence development of conceptions, clarity of conceptions, and assurance that conceptions are relatively adequate all appear to be involved in the nature of oughtness.

i. All involve objectification of ideas; i.e., about what one's alternatives are, about what his obligation is, about what course of

action or inaction should be taken, and about
what kinds of consequences may be expected.
If one has reified his ideas of values at stake,
then he is more likely to reify also his conception of his obligation. He may say to himself: "I really do have this obligation even
though I wish that I didn't have it." Reification is more likely when others are involved
and when one believes that others share his conception of what his obligation is. Understanding of oughtness involves all of those problems
previously summarized in discussing naive, scientific and pragmatic realistic theories of
knowledge.[10] Among the problems pressing persons responsible for guiding others is how to
prevent them from being too naively realistic
about their obligations and then, after discovering essentially subjective aspects of obligations,
from shifting too completely to a view that obligations are purely subjective, completely ar-
bitrary, or foolish illusions. Maintenance of
a pragmatic attitude toward finding out how
much both subjective and real factors condition
each particular ought seems called for.

   j. All are forward-looking. Actual obligations involve present feelings, but the are conceived in such a way that present decisions will
have future consequences. One may now believe
that he ought to have done differently in the
past; and he may now believe that he ought to
make restitution for a past mistake. He may,
therefore, now believe that he did in the past
have an obligation which he did not fulfill;
but this results from his reification of ideas
about obligation which can be reified as if
past, present or future. One may now believe
that by deciding now to marry, for example, he
will have future obligations, some of which he
may and some of which he may not now know. But
regardless of whether or how reified, expecta-
tion of future consequences, no matter how

unclearly conceived, seem implicit in every
feeling of oughtness.

k. All involve feelings of compulsion. The
power involved is not physical, though un-
critical minds may fail to distinguish one kind
of compulsion from another, and those unfortunate to have acquired their views about the nature of oughtness from childhood spankings may
habitually regard the compulsion experienced
in feelings of oughtness as akin to or not
much different from those experienced when
physical force is applied to prod or prevent
their action. Unfortunately also, the fre-
quency with which negative commands and cor-
poral punishment condition early experiences
of oughtness cause some to conceive oughtness
wholly in negative terms. "Stop this!" "Don't
do that!" "That's wrong." "You ought not...!"
Our analysis of the ultimate locus of the compulsory power felt as oughtness points to intrinsic values, both enjoyments and sufferings;
and although further studies may show that
suffering more often and more effectively
motivates feelings of oughtness than enjoyments, I believe that ethics as a science
proves more servicable when its theories are
worked out in terms of positive values or,
better, both positive and negative values,
than when negative values are stressed as
primary. Surely students approach the subject more rationally when appeals are made to
positive, or both positive and negative, values
than when appeals are made in ways that such
childhood fears and ruthless environments
prejudicially inhibit relatively objective
approaches.

l. All involve feelings of agency. Will
or intention, already mentioned, involves
accepting one's self as an agent or actor.
Unfortunately, some who approach ethics as a
science regard its subject matter as mores,

and therefore as a branch of anthropology, and
study behavior in terms of conformity or nonconformity to customary behavior patterns. The
commonness or peculiarity of such behavior patterns are taken as the primary substance to be
investigated. But moral action from the view-
point of the actor involves problems, choices,
decisions and actions not only in which his own
welfare is at stake but for which he is the
actor, i.e., chooser, the decider, the executer.
Accepting oneself as an agent presupposes accepting one's self as existing, and some conception of self. Such conception may be vague
or clear, simple or complex, and of one's self
as rigid or flexible. The importance of conceptions of self for understanding the nature
of oughtness leads me to devote the next chapter
to the nature of a self which acts as an agent.

Agency connotes power to initiate. An act
of will involves some notion of self-activity.
No matter what theory of causation one accepts
— i.e.,, whether will is causally determined
completely, is completely uncaused, or is partly caused — a feeling of agency as self-activity seems an essential condition to experiencing
feelings of oughtness. A person in catatonia
or deep sleep is not regarded as an agent, and
surely he has no actual oughtness, no matter
what his potentialities.

m. All involve feelings of commitment. Such
commitment is of two sorts, namely, to choose
or decide and to act on one's decision or to
carry out one's intentions. The distinction
between them may not arise in awareness, especially when need for instant decision and action
are called for. At other times, the distinction
not only is clear but performance of the two
functions becomes widely separated, as when
governments establish separate legislative and
adminstrative branches for the special purposes
of choosing among alternatives and reaching

policy decisions to which the state thereby
commits itself, on the one hand, and of putting
into practice, sometimes through laborious,
lasting and costly efforts, the decisions
reached, on the other.

The commitments involved in feelings of
oughtness vary greatly. They may arise and
subside in a moment of anger, or they may be
long in forming, as in choosing a career, and
may be long in execution, as when marriage contracts require intention to continue "until
death do us part" or even "throughout time and
eternity." They may pertain to trivial issues,
as when deciding to move right or left in a
checker game, or to one's whole life, as in an
oath of allegiance when joining military service. They may be extremely general, as when
a college dean or president agrees to be responsible for whatever unforeseen situations
require, or extremely limited, as when insurance policies stipulate precise conditions for
liability and exact amounts of payments due.
They may function as implicit in one's behavior,
as when approaching another without hostile
warning conveys intention not to harm, or they
may require strict conformity to preestablished
ritual, as when a president takes an oath of
office or when a "last will and testament" requires formal signature by a notary public
before witnesses who can testify that the sign-
er is "in full possession of his mental powers."
They may occur as highly conditional, e.g.
"If Mary gets here in time and has enough
money, then we will go to the movie if Walt
Disney's Bambi is on," or utterly unconditional, e.g., "I will see to it that your Dad gets
you a bicycle, even if I have to pay for it
myself."

Notice that commitment to carry out decisions
over a period of time involve a commitment to
future commitments, since as time goes on one

may face, on each new relevant occasion, the
problem of whether to continue to carry out
the previous commitment. Some commitments are
regarded as irrevocable and hence precommitting
all future choices. Others are regarded as con-
tingent in the sense that, although no change
in policy is intended, if unforeseen circumstances prevent carrying out the decision, then
a new decision must be reached about what modifications in the commitment are required and/or
permissible. Long-range personal commitments,
i.e., of the sort involved when a person decides
to live his life in a certain way, then tend
to behave as character traits; since some kinds
of commitments are essential for some kinds of
professions, we can sometimes judge something
about a person's commitments and conceptions
of his obligations by the kind of profession
in which he is engaged.

n. All involve potentiality as well as actu-
ality. I do not assert that potentiality, either
that causing the feeling of oughtness or its
potentiality for influencing consequences, must
be present in awareness. But since what is
actual could not have become actual unless
there existed that which brought it into existence, potentiality clearly is involved. Examination of this condition, and many others,
will be postponed to the following section on
"Conditional Oughtness," where "conditional
potentiality" will seem more obviously relevant.[11]

2. Intentions. Complications involved in
understanding intentions, one of the foregoing
essential conditions of actual oughts, call for
examination and additional hypotheses. Although
intention may be experienced as simple and even
as transparent in the sense that one may intend
without being aware that he is intending, analysis reveals at least three factors commonly
calling for explanation by ethical scientists:
(a) Volition or will. (b) What is intended.

50

(c) Degrees of intention.

a. Volition or will. A person cannot choose
without intending to choose. Can a person experience an ought to choose without actually
choosing? Except when sudden death, cessation
of consciousness, or loss of energy to continue
attending to an ought before one actually
chooses, each actual ought normally embodies
intention or volition.[12]

Volition or will is a topic fraught with
misunderstandings. It is very complex and
intermingled with other problems, most of which
cannot be explored here. A main problem, "Is
the will free?" is shrouded in culturally inherited, widely-held mistaken views about freedom and determinism. For example, many believe
that whatever is caused or determined is not
free. They hold that since nothing happens
without being caused to happen in the way that
it does happen, there can be no freedom. And
since ethical choices presuppose freedom, there
can be no ethical choices and no ethics and,
of course, no science of ethics. Such a view
is false because it presupposes that freedom
is not caused. In fact, when we are unfree we
are caused to be unfree and when we are free
we are caused to be free. If freedom is not
absence of causation, then what is it?

A person is free whenever he is able to do
what he wants to do. His wants are caused and
his abilities are caused, and whenever his wants
and his abilities are fitted to each other he
is free.[13] What is important for ethics is the
feeling of freedom. When a person is aware of
himself as an agent freely choosing between
alternatives, the compulsion constituting oughtness appears to have its source in the apparently greater good. But when he feels forced to
choose a ham sandwich instead of a cheese sandwich which he prefers, because another person
claims to be unable to eat ham, for example,

51

then one feels unfree to choose what he prefers. Involved in this example is another
choice, whether or not to accomodate the other
person. This choice may have been made freely,
especially if the person enjoys being accomo-
dating. But if this choice was made grudging-
ly, then involved is a desire not to be faced
with such a choice.

Actual oughts, except those terminated abnormally, involve choosing and thus intending
and willing. One's will is not always free,
because one does not always get what he wants.
Often he gets only part of what he wants; then
his will is only partly free. The causes determining his situation cause him to be only
partly free. But actual oughts, except those
terminated abnormally, involve volition or
will regardless of the extent to which each
particular ought and volition are free.

One of the hypotheses explicitly proposed
here is that nothing happens without being
caused to happen in the way that it does happen. Another hypothesis is that one's will is
free whenever one is able to do what one wants
to do. This is genuine freedom. Another hypothesis: All persons have much genuine freedom part of the time. Another hypothesis: No
person attains all that he wants; no persons
are free all of the time. A deduction from
the foregoing hypotheses may be stated as an
hypothesis: Genuine freedom and unfreedom
of will are caused.[14]

b. What is intended? Each actual ought is
shaped in terms of concepts, vague or clear, of
how the alternatives appear. Unclarity or uncertainty regarding the appearances function
as uncertainties regarding an intention resulting from a choice. Since a person both
intends to choose (to choose as he feels compelled to choose) and intends to act in whatever consequential way his choice calls for,

what he chooses and what action follows im-
plicitly from such choice is a part of his intending. I am not aware that there are any
limitations on what one may intend as part of
an actual ought. At least I propose as an
initial hypothesis that ethics as a science
does not presuppose any limitations on what
may be intended in any actual ought. It may
be that, after a study of better and worse
intentions, generalizations (conditional
oughts) about what ought not be intended may
be developed and established.[15]

c. Degrees of intention. Although at times
we distinguish sharply between intended and un-
intended actions, at other times we are unsure.
Many different kinds of factors contribute to
such uncertainty.

For example, when we cannot foresee all of
the consequences that will follow from a choice
or act, do we intend to cause all of the consequences? If not, when we intend only part
of the consequences, is our intention a partial
intention? Or do we sometimes feel fully committed to our choice even when consequences
are uncertain? Does such commitment involve
risk, or gambling, in the sense that we intend
consequences of which we are uncertain? The
more we learn about life, the more complicated
it appears and the more we recognize that we
cannot take all of the consequential factors
into consideration. Does more such knowledge
require increasing the risk, or gambling, aspect
of our intentions?

Sometimes we are quite indifferent to choices
that confront us and assent only "half-heartedly"
or permissively. In some situations we "can't
be othered" and intentionally refuse to choose.
Can one intend not to intend? When so, are any
of the consequences of one's not intending part
of what he intends? Sometimes the emotional
intensity of our feelings when we intend is

much greater than at other times. Do we intend
more fully when we are more enthusiastic or
angry than when calm and unemotional? Do hyper-
thyroid people intend more fully than those
who are ill or weak or subthyroid? Understanding the nature of actual oughtness includes
recognizing variations in such degrees of intention.

Thus far we have considered the intention
of a single act of choice. A more bothersome
problem is the fact that most acts of choice
are parts of a series of choices in which the
later choices made in light of previously un-
considered factors require modifications in
what is intended. How much, if any, of such
modified intention should be attributable to
the first intention? Must we at times intend
to have our intentions modified by successive
intentions? The problem becomes even more complicated when a person intends to share in a
common decision with other persons and when he
is not entirely clear how others conceive the
decision and when successive experiences by
each participant are subject at least somewhat
to their own modifications. The problem becomes
still more intricate when one intends to assent
to future decisions by representatives acting
as officers of institutionalized groups about
problems that have not yet occurred.

I raise the foregoing questions about degrees
of intentions and uncertainties regarding intentions as a reminder of some of the complexities
that must be faced in ethics as a science. Each
actual ought, although often unitary and simple
in its particular occurrence, may also be very
complicated in nature and conditions in ways
that can be studied scientifically.

3. Conscience. The word "conscience" is
used in referring to both a feeling of oughtness, or ought-not-ness, and to a tendency
established in persons to produce such a feel-

ing. As a feeling of oughtness, conscience
seems to me to have a negative aspect properly
described as fear. This negative aspect operates whenever we become aware that we have
chosen, are choosing, or are in danger of
choosing a lesser rather than a greater good
or a greater evil rather than a lesser evil.
Whenever the differences in values of alternatives are unclear, so that one cannot be sure
that he is choosing the greater good, he may
fear that he is not choosing as he ought.
Whenever the values of the alternatives appear
so similar that one is reluctant to not choose
the lesser, he may fear that abandonment of
the almost equally great good of the lesser
alternative constitutes some kind of evil.
Conscience operates as a feeling of fear that
one will not attain the results intended. Conscience operates frequently when one faces
conflicts of interests.

How conscience originates is an additional
problem that will not detain us here.[16] My
present hypothesis about the nature of conscience is that, although it often occurs as an
actual ought-not, it is by nature an ought
with a negative factor added, which negative
factor functions more or less (i.e., as a matter of degree) as fear that one will not choose,
and act, wisely. The greater the apparent values at stake and the greater the uncertainty regarding assurance of correct choice the more intense the feeling of fear. Although much conscience results from social conditioning, some
is purely private, as when one fears that he
has swallowed poison instead of tonic, and
some is instinctive, as when one suddenly
fears falling off a cliff.

I do not propose that conscience is essential to oughtness. I believe that persons
often face choices between alternatives with
complete confidence and without any feeling

of fear. Yet, whenever a person is faced with uncertainities (and these tend to increase as life becomes more richly complicated), the tendency to experience concern that choices are not always best persists. Such tendency, which often manifests itself as anxiety, may be regarded as conscience, a low-intensity feeling that may increase in intensity whenever evidence of failure appears. So, although conscience is not essential to oughtness, much of a person's experience of actual oughtness tends to be suffused with conscience.

CONDITIONAL OUGHTNESS

1. Nature of conditional oughtness. A conditional ought is something that a person ought to choose or ought to do if all of certain **specified** conditions occur. An actual ought, one being felt presently as a compulsion to choose the apparently better of two alternatives, exists because all of the causes or conditions of its existence did cooperate in causing it. A conditional ought is one which would, or could, become an actual ought if and when all other needed conditions cooperate in actualizing it.

The oughtness of a conditional ought is derived from its apparent potentiality for contributing to some actual ought. Although not all conditional oughts become actualized, the apparent possibility for a condition to contribute to and participate in some actual ought is the reason for attributing conditional oughtness to it. Since a person does not know all of the causes and conditions of his actual oughts, those that he does not know cannot become apparent bases for the conditional oughts that he does know. Since some conditions of actual oughts may remain unknown to all human beings, they cannot become apparent conditions

56

for actual oughts for anyone.

How do conditional oughts come to attention? In many different ways. Some arise out of personal experience. "I stub my toe every time I walk through your room in the dark. So I ought to turn on the light when I walk through your room after dark." Some are expressed by parents. "If you cross the heavily trafficed street alone, you may get killed. So, if you do not want to get killed, then you ought not cross the heavily trafficed street without adult guidance." Some are induced by peer groups. "Last one in the pool is a...." Some emerge in social experience. "Persons who smile are more approachable. So, if you want to be more approachable, smile." Some persist in folk culture. "Early to bed and early to rise makes a person healthy, wealthy and wise. So, if you want to be healthy, wealthy or wise, then go to bed early and rise early." Some continue to be indoctrinated from ancient sources. "Honor thy father and thy mother that thy days may be long upon the land which the Lord thy God giveth thee."[18] So, if you want "that thy days be long in the land...," then you ought to honor father and mother.

Some result from group decisions. "All in favor of $10 for membership dues say 'aye.' Passed. So, if you want to be a member, then you ought to pay $10." Some result from legislation, local, state, national, etc. All enacted laws are normally intended to function as conditional oughts. Policy decisions often are intended to serve as conditional oughts. Some develop from scientific investigation. Laws of nature discovered by scientists are not conditional oughts, but each one may serve as a basis for conditional oughts. "Water boils at 212 degrees Fahrenheit at sea level under normal atmospheric pressure. So, if you want to boil water at sea level under normal

57

atmospheric pressure, then you ought to heat
it to 212 degrees Fahrenheit." Some are acquired from literature, movies or other media,
accidentally or through formal instruction.
Some occur because a person struggles with a
problem and has "figured it out for himself."
Some originate from many other sources.

One major difficulty in understanding, recognizing and utilizing conditional oughts is that
too often they have been stated unconditionally.
An excited parent cries "Never cross that street
alone!" Soon the same parent teaches the child
how to cross the street alone. "Honor thy
father and thy mother," abstracted from the
conditions of living long in the land, has been
been preached as a commandment without exceptions. Legislators, ignorant of appropriate
exceptions, often enact laws as without exceptions. Hasty laboratory instructors, ingoring
altitude and atmospheric pressure, assert: "To
boil water, you must heat it to 212 degrees
Fahrenheit." Much distrust of ethics results
from misstating conditional oughts as unconditional. A major service of ethics as a science
can be to clarify the distinction and to emphasize its importance.

2. Kinds of conditional oughts. The numbers
and kinds of conditions that can function as
bases for conditional oughts range from a single
condition, at one extreme, to all of the conditions of existence, at the other extreme, with
endless numbers of specific kinds of conditions
between these extremes. These numbers and kinds
will be sampled by considering some conditions
for particular actual oughts, some common to all
actual oughts, and some for each kind of actual
ought.

a. Conditions for particular actual oughts.
Sometimes a person is aware of only one particular condition preventing actualization of commitment to an ought. "I'll buy this candy, if

you'll loan me a dime." If no dime is loaned, an actual ought to buy the candy does not exist. The conditional ought, in this example, "I ought to buy this candy if you will loan me a dime," is not only particular but also singular. A person may be aware of two, three, four or many particular conditions for the actualization of an ought. "I will give you an A in Math. II if you complete all of the exercizes, get all of the answers correct, and get the work done legibly before Friday."

A person may be aware of a single universal condition that may prevent actualization of commitment to an ought. A universal condition is one common to all actual oughts. All of the conditions essential to existence on earth are essential conditions of the existence of actual oughts on earth. If discontinuance of the earth and all that exists on it is a possibility to consider relative to a particular prospective actual ought, then a person aware of this possibility is aware of a universal conditional ought relative to it. "I will meet you in London on Monday if that approaching comet does not destroy the earth." A person may also be aware of several universal conditions that may prevent actualization of a particular ought. The point being made here is that conditional oughts of which a person is aware relative to particular actual oughts may be either particular or universal, and also that, therefore, not all conditional oughts are universals. In the following two sections, we shall be concerned almost entirely with universals, either those common to all actual oughts or those common to all actual oughts of each kind.

b. Conditions common to all actual oughts. In addition to the essential conditions of actual oughts mentioned above (pp. 43-49), several other common conditions of all actual oughts may be noted.

(1) All of the conditions common to all existences are conditions of the existence of
actual oughts. The scientific task of deciding
what conditions are common to all existences
belongs elsewhere. It is the task of metaphy-
sicians and of sciences facing problems about
such universal characteristics of existence.
For example, can anything exist apart from
space, time, change, relation or causation?[19]
If not, then these are conditions of the existence of actual oughts. These conditions of
existence do not function as bases for conditional oughts unless a person becomes aware of
them and of how they may be relevant to prospective obligations. "Professor Jones says the
universe began with a big bang and will end
suddenly in the silence of a big black hole.
I'll pay you back on Saturday unless we reach
the end of time."

(2) All of the conditions common to all existences on earth are conditions of the existence of actual oughts (flying astronauts ex-
cepted?). For example, gravity conditions the
bodies of all persons and in this way conditions the existence of actual oughts in persons.
Gravity does not function as a basis for a conditional ought unless a person becomes aware of
its relevance to some choice in prospect. "Be
careful on that hill. If you slip with that
heavy load, you will surely fall and hurt your-
self." Principles of geology and geography may
all serve as bases for conditional oughts. Thus
ethics as a science regards increasing knowledge
of such principles, both through further research
and through further education of people, as useful for increasing the beneficial results of
ethical choices taking them into account.

(3) All conditions common to all living
beings are conditions of the existence of actual oughts in live persons. Again these condi-

tions may be ignored as irrelevant to many
actual oughts. But they too may become bases
for conditional oughts. For example, a person
cannot live long without breathing. When a
person dies, all of his actual oughts cease.
While living, a person wanting to continue to
live often becomes aware that air pollution
or lack of exercize may endanger his breathing.
When so, knowledge of biological and physiological principles of healthy lungs can function
as bases for conditional oughts. "If you want
to live longer, then you ought to exercise
more."

(4) All conditions common to conscious
beings are conditions of the existence of
actual oughts which cannot occur without awareness. So all principles of psychology, including physiological psychology, relevant to understanding the consciousness essential for actual
oughts may serve as bases for conditional oughts.
"If you drink, don't drive."

(5) All of the conditions common to, especially those essential to, human association may
be conditions for the existence of actual oughts
involving human association. All such conditions
of human existence may serve as bases for conditional oughts. "We cannot have children as
long as you are stationed in the Arctic." "If
a family wants legitimate children, then husband
and wife ought to associate intimately."

Many other kinds of conditions essential to
the existence of actual oughts have been neglected here. Regarding all of them, they may function
as bases for conditional oughts when they appear
relevant to alternatives appearing in choices.
The sciences that inform us of the universal
characteristics of existence, of existence on
earth, of life, of consciousness, and of human
association are not as such ethical sciences.
But their information may serve as bases for
conditional oughts whenever it becomes relevant

to choosing between alternatives.²⁰

to choosing between alternatives.[20]

c. Conditions for each kind of actual ought.
Things exist in kinds. Each kind of thing has
its own kind of nature. Those kinds of things
that have become comparatively stable, including
having comparatively stable kinds of processes,
often become objects of study. More general
kinds have been grouped into subjects for the
physical, biological and social sciences. More
specific kinds have been grouped as subjects
for physics, chemistry, astronomy, geology,
geography and physical sciences. More specific
kinds are investigated by molecular physics,
atomic physics, nuclear physics, etc. In addition to the pure sciences, we have technologies,
both general and more specialized, and other
applied sciences including engineering of all
kinds. The list of kinds of industries, professions, trades, occupations, kinds of pro-
ducts, kinds of services needed is lengthy, and
newer kinds seem to develop every day.

The point of the above summary of kinds of
things is that each, in having its own nature,
has conditions essential to its nature about
which principles can be stated. Each such principle may serve as a basis for a conditional
ought. So the numbers and kinds of potential
conditional oughts seem practically beyond
countability. Yet each is available as something that may be a primary determining factor
in values apparent to choosers. Thus each has
potential ethical significance. The importance
of such potential significance is something that
should not be overlooked by ethical scientists.
The more fully developed ethics as a science
becomes, the more important the significance of
principles about the natures of kinds as bases
for conditional oughts will become.

Although we shall mention only a few "Other
Ethical Sciences" in Chapter V, the roles, potential and actual, of all of the other sciences in

dealing with subjects contributing to ethical decisions should not be underestimated. The problem of the ethical significance of knowledge of the nature of kinds has taken shape through processes of increasing specialization. Each specialist who achieves competence in understanding his field thereby becomes an authority of what is best in his field. As one who knows what is best, he thereby becomes the ethical authority in his field. Not only do we have specialized kinds of ethics, but each specialist is himself also a specialized ethicist to the extent that he knows what is best in his specialty. Growth in specialization thus involves growth in specialized ethics.

Of course, if a specialist isolates himself from other specialists and from larger processes within which his specialty functions, he may foster a kind of ignorance also having ethical consequences. I have dealt with the issues regarding the nature of specialization and the philosophy of the specialist, both narrower and broader specialism, elsewhere and will not repeat them here.[21] But here I must say that, competent or incompetent, every specialist is something of an ethicist. Thus ethicists concerned with ethics as a science have natural interests in increasing the competence of specialists as ethicists in general as well as in their specialzied ethics.

3. Some principles for choosing. For convenience in writing, I have ignored in the foregoing the fact that some conditional oughts, namely, those stated as general principles, should also be stated as conditional for purposes of precision and clarity. Accepting as a fact that water boils at 212 degrees Fahrenheit at sea level under normal atmospheric pressure, this principle may be stated as a conditional ought: "If and when you desire to boil water at sea level under normal atmospheric

pressure, then, other things being equal, you ought to heat the water to 212 degrees Fahrenheit." The phrase, "other things being equal," meaning by other things all other conditions, is part of what is meant by each principle as a conditional ought. Careful scientists, seeking precision of statement, always include this phrase or some equivalent, so careful ethical scientists ought to do the same.

Persons practicing ethics in the sense of employing principles as conditional oughts in making choices ought to keep this important conditional nature of conditional oughts in mind whenever possible. In discussing the nature of conditional oughts above, I mentioned that distrust of ethics results from mistaking conditional oughts as unconditional. Now I point out further that failure to keep the "other things being equal" universal condition of principles as conditional oughts exemplfies the same mistake.

The present section is devoted to stating some principles for choosing that appear to me to hold universally, i.e., for all people at all times who understand them clearly, as conditional oughts. That is, they hold universally all other things being equal at the time when they participate in an actual ought. Each principle and the whole set of principles are proposed here as hypotheses for consideration and testing by anyone who chooses to do so. To me, these principles seem obvious, I propose them, further, as principles accepted in ethics as an established science. They are arranged for convenience into five groups.[22]

a. Principles applying to both intrinsic and instrumental values. Our first general principle is that, other things being equal, when faced with a choice between two alternatives, one of which is good and the other evil, a person ought always choose the good alternative. The prin-

ciple consists in the good (ultimately, the
intrinsic good) being the ultimate locus of
power for compelling our choices.

The phrase, "other things being equal,"
applies not only to the principle under consideration here but to all of the principles
for choosing which follow.

A second general principle petains to alternatives consisting in greater and lesser
goods and to alternatives consisting in greater and lesser evils. This will be considered
in three aspects. The first aspect may be
stated as follows: When faced with the problem of choosing between two alternatives, one
of which is good and the other better, other
things being equal, one ought always choose
the better. The second aspect may be stated
as follows: When faced with the problem of
choosing between two alternatives, one of
which is bad and the other worse, other things
being equal, one ought always choose the bad
rather than the worse. The third aspect,
which combines and extends the first two aspects,
may be stated as follows: When faced with a
problem of choosing between two or more alternatives, some of which are better than others
and some of which are worse than others, other
things being equal, one ought always choose
the most good and the least evil possible.

These three aspects have their explanation
in the general principle that, of two goods
(ultimately two intrinsic goods) one of which
is better than the other, the greater goodness
of the one has within itself the power to compel our will to choose it, and that, of two
evils (ultimately two intrinsic evils) one of
which is worse that the other, the greater
evil in the one has within itself the power
to compel our will to choose to avoid it.

We might note that the first principle
stated above has been incorporated in the

statement of the third aspect. The inclusion
of simpler principles in more complex principles
does not eliminate them, though it may eliminate
need for enumerating them. Rather such inclusion indicates not only that complex principles
depend on simpler ones but also that simpler
ones which exist as statements based on partial
similarities between situations involve, and are
involved in, the more complex principles needed
to complete their own nature and contribution to
an interpretation and codification of general
principles for choosing that is adequate to account for the more complex similarities existing between situations.

   b. Principles pertaining primarily to intrinsic values. The options confronted with respect
to the problem of choosing among alternative intrinsic values (a problem that does not arise
for one wholly immersed in enjoyment of intrinsic value) have to do with actualizing intrinsic
values or with more fully appreciating intrinsic
values only partly actualized. To the extent
that all intrinsic goods may be experienced as
"enjoyments" — such as feelings of pleasure,
enthusiasm, satisfaction, contentment or any
blending of these — rules for choosing can be
formulated.

   To the extent that enjoyments differ in
"quantity," when faced with the problem of
choosing between greater or lesser quantity,
other things being equal, one ought always
choose the greater quantity. If the enjoyments
differ in "duration," when faced with the problem of choosing between longer and shorter durations of an enjoyment, other things being
equal, one ought always choose the longer-last-
ing enjoyment. When they differ in "intensity,"
when faced with a problem of choosing betwee a
more intense and a less intense enjoyment, other
things being equal, one ought always choose the
more intense enjoyment. When they differ in

"quality," when faced with the problem of
choosing between a higher quality and a lower
quality enjoyment, other things being equal,
one ought always choose the higher quality
enjoyment.

Since, during a particular period in which
prospective enjoyments are to be experienced,
they may have both quantitative, durational,
intensive and qualitative aspects, the issue
normally becomes one of whether to choose
quantity versus duration, duration versus intensity, intensity versus quality, or, rather,
between more complex (e.g., quantity-intensity
versus duration-quality) alternatives. Since
situations normally also contain awareness of
objects or object-complexes and activities or
activity-complexes, choice problems regard the
above-outlined alternatives seldom appear to
sharply defined. Vagueness, uncertainty, even
ignorance, regarding such issues leave us vic-
tims of whim, impulse or inclination. Nevertheless, the foregoing principles for choosing
among enjoyments should appear, upon reflection,
as naturally reasonable conditional oughts.
Although "other things" are seldom if ever equal,
awareness of the availability of such principles
may provide both additional assurance (and enjoyment in being a person who can, if he chooses,
choose on principle, which enjoyment itself may
be experienced as an intrinsic value) and actual assistance whenever issues do occur in sharp-
ened form. The principles are significant also
because they carry over into decisions regarding
the making of instruments. Ought we manufacture
instruments that produce more quantity, duration,
intensity or quality of enjoyments? These principles bear also on how we feel that we ought
to treat our friends, for we may rightly choose
to tickle a child, praise a youth, evidence
fidelity to a spouse, and sit quietly conversing
about life with an oldster, whereas reversing

these options could have quite different effects.

c. Principles pertaining primarily to instrumental values. (1) When faced with the problem of choosing between means which are essential to life and means which are not essential to life, other things being equal, one ought always choose the means which are essential to life. The reasoning underlying this principle is that more intrinsic value will exist if life exists than if it does not exist. However, if the life expected will be one of greater evil than of intrinsic good, then, other things being equal, one ought to choose means essential to ending such life.

(2) By applying our "second general principle" cited above (i.e., other things being equal, one ought choose the most good and least evil possible) to problems pertaining primarily to choosing among instrumental values, we may note some typical subprinciples. Three will be noted, namely, those dealing with permanent versus transient instruments, those dealing with productive versus unproductive instruments, and those dealing with efficient versus inefficient instruments.

(a) When faced with the problem of choosing between two instruments, one of which is more enduring as a potential instrumental good, other things being equal, one ought always choose the more enduring in preference to the less enduring good.

(b) When faced with the problem of choosing between two instruments, one of which is more more productive in the sense that it is useful in producing more instruments which can produce still more instruments, etc., which function as potential instrumental goods, other things being equal, one ought always choose the more productive in preference to the less productive.

(c) When faced with the problem of choosing

between two instruments, one of which is more
efficient in the sense that it produces, directly or indirectly, more intrinsic good than
it involves evil in its production, and the
other which is less efficient, then, other
things being equal, one ought always choose
the former.

Regarding each of these three general subprinciples we may note that, although distin-
guishable, they are also similar in pertaining
to more versus less instrumental good, in over-
lapping with respect to the instruments to
which they apply, and in finding their justification in the common underlying principle
which consists in long-range interests, i.e.,
what is best for one's self in the long run.
Each is a form of the principle that Bentham
called "fecundity." Each has a negative coun-
terpart which together may be stated as a
general code item: "Avoid waste." All may refer to instruments existing either outside or
inside self; i.e., to things external to self
("opportunities") and to character traits,
habits, energies ("capacities"); or to both
("abilities") and their fitness to each other.
These three principles may be stated together
as: When faced with the problem of choosing
between two alternatives, one of which increases
and the other of which decreases one's abilities
in the long run, other things being equal, one
ought always choose the former. All may be involved in a shift in the ratio of significance
of the permanent versus the transient, or the
productive versus the unproductive, and the
more versus the less efficient as one's life
proceeds; for if one has much life yet to live,
he may rightly be more concerned about enduring
and productive goods than later in life, unless,
and to the extent that, he expects himself to
live on, in any of his levels of being, as
identified with his children, his creations,

his nation, his culture, mankind, or the universe itself.

(3) Another issue regarding instrumental values has to do with the relative certainty or uncertainty that a potential instrumental good will become actualized and result in actual enjoyment of intrinsic value. This third issue may be stated as follows: When faced with the problem of choosing between two instrumental goods, one of which is more sure to result in   actual intrinsic good and the other of which is less sure, other things being equal, one ought always choose the former. For example, a knife that is known to be sharp and sure to cut should be preferred to one that is dull and that may or may not cut, other things being equal. Or a brand of product that has always pleased should be chosen in preference to a new brand that is yet to be tried, other things being equal. A kind of activity that has always yielded enjoyment should be favored against one that sometimes does and sometimes does not bring enjoyment, other things being equal. This issue and these examples have negative counterparts. For example, a kind of activity that has always resulted in boredom should be avoided in preference to a kind of activity in which prospects regarding boredom remain uncertain, other things being equal.

d. Principles for choosing between intrinsic and instrumental values. Three general principles will be distinguished.

(1) When faced with the problem of choosing between two alternatives, one of which is an intrinsic good and the other of which is an instrumental good, other things being equal, one ought always choose the intrinsic good. The phrase "other things being equal" is important here especially because the conditional ought being stated is highly abstract and because a seemingly instrumental good is not

actually an instrumental good unless it actually results in an intrinsic good. Thus, if the intrinsic good involved in this instrumental good also becomes part of the perspective within which the alternatives are viewed, then the problem becomes that of choosing between one intrinsic good on the one hand and an instrumental good together with its potential intrinsic good on the other. Many actual choices must be made between an immediately enjoyable intrinsic good and obtaining instruments whose prospects of fruitfulness remain uncertain. Here the issue of certainty versus uncertainty regarding instruments resulting in actual intrinsic goods becomes paramount. For example, one may feel a need for deciding between spending his last now-available dollar for a highly praised movie, the enjoyment of which is immediate and self-terminating, as against spending it for an otherwise unobtainable highly rated book that he may never find time to read. Of course, since "other things" are seldom "equal," pride in owning such a book as well as prospective discomfort arising from needs for caring for it, storing it, dusting it, guarding it against theft, may be factors.

The foregoing discussion, focusing on difficulties in taking the principle into consideration as such in actual decisions, should not becloud its basicness to value theory and ethics. The principle is already inherent in the distinction (and in the need for distinguishing) between intrinsic and instrumental value in the first place. Hence, insofar as one can choose between an actual intrinsic good which is an end in itself and an instrumental good which does not have its end in itself, one ought to choose the former because intrinsic good is both the ultimate basis of choice and is intuitively apprehended as ultimate or as an end-in-itself whenever its

nature is clearly recognized. Intrinsic good
is "the end that justifies the means" and thus
ought always to be preferred to the means,
other things being equal.

(2) The second principle, which may seem to
contradict the first, is really a necessary supplement to it. Whereas instrumental good depends on intrinsic good teleologically (intrinsic good is the end for which instrumental good
is the means), intrinsic good depends for its
existence upon instrumental good causally. Hence,
to the extent that an intrinsic good cannot exist without those instruments and their goods
as causes of it, one must treat the instruments
and their goods as prior to the intrinsic good
to be caused. This principle may be stated as
follows: When, and in so far as, instrumental
good is causally prior to intrinsic good, other
things being equal, one ought always choose the
instrumental good or means to an end (thus obtaining both means and end) as against an end,
or intrinsic good, which does not, because it
cannot, exist without the means to it. These
two principles do not contradict each other because the phrase, "other things being equal,"
contained in each of them, signifies, in part,
that the factors stated in the other are thereby being taken into account.

(3) The third general principle incorporates
the first two in a more comprehensive statement:
When faced with the problem of choosing between
two alternatives, one of which consists of both
intrinsic good and instrumental good and the
other of which consists in either intrinsic
good or instrumental good alone, other things
being equal, one ought always choose the former.

e. Principles for choosing between intrinsic
and instrumental values where production and consumption are at stake. Using the term "enjoyed"
and "not enjoyed" to refer to experiences in
which intrinsic goods are present and absent,

respectively (principles relative to intrinsic evils are neglected here), I propose the following:

(1) When faced with the problem of choosing described in the following, other things being equal, one ought to choose the first alternative: (a) Productive activity which is enjoyed and productive activity which is not enjoyed. (b) Consumptive activity which is enjoyed and consumptive activity which is not enjoyed. (c) Activity which is both productive and consumptive and enjoyed and activity which is both productive and consumptive and not enjoyed.

(2) When faced with the problem of choosing described in the following, other things being equal, one ought to choose the first alternative: (a) Productive activity which is enjoyed and consumptive activity which is enjoyed (equally). (b) Nonconsumptive activity which is enjoyed and consumptive activity which is enjoyed. (c) Activity which is both productive and nonconsumptive which is enjoyed and activity which is both consumptive and nonproductive which is enjoyed. One ought to choose the first in each case because, in addition to the enjoyments, presumed to be equal, instruments that may have value later are produced, not consumed, or produced and not consumed, respectively.

(3) Still more complex situations exist which, because they are the same in some respects, provide a basis for formulating principles. Some of these involve "diminishing returns." There is a sense in which all "laws of diminishing returns" are ethical laws to the extent that instrumental goods are involved. The first has to do with diminishing returns (i.e., actual intrinsic goods enjoyed) resulting from increasing production of instruments. When a point has been reached at which additional production can result in no more enjoyment, then an "ought to produce" turns into an "ought not

to produce," other things being equal (i.e.,
do not make instruments that can never be used,
when no enjoyment can come from making them).
The second has to do with diminishing returns
resulting from increasing consumption of instruments. When a point has been reached at which
additional consumption of instruments yields
no more enjoyment, then an "ought to consume"
turns into an "ought not to consume," other
things being equal (e.g., do not eat more candy
now if taste buds are completely saturated or
if appetite is perfectly satiated). The third
has to do with diminishing returns resulting
from both increasing production and increasing
consumption of instruments. When a point has
been reached in the production and consumption
of instruments at which additional production
and consumption of instruments yields no additional enjoyment, an "ought to produce and consume" turns into an "ought not to produce and
consume," other things being equal.

APPARENT VERSUS "REAL" OUGHTNESS

Problems concerning the common distinction
between appearance and reality, or between how
things appear and how they "really are," recurs
relative to oughtness. Oughtness, as the power
that an apparently greater good has over an apparently lesser good in compelling our choices,
is defined in terms of apparent goodness. A
person who wants what is best, wants not what
merely appears best but what is "really best."
Thus anyone aware of the distinction will naturally propose that "Oughtness consists not in
choosing a merely apparent greater good over
a merely apparent lesser good but in choosing
a really greater good over a really lesser good.
This is real oughtness, and it really ought to
be preferred to merely apparent oughtness."

1. Difficulties with the distinction. The
distinction between apparent and real oughtness is fraught with many difficulties.

a. Ambiguities of the word "real." Mean-
ings of the word "real" vary so much that I
have hesitated to introduce the distinction.
In addition to popular varieties, technical
differences related to epistemology, metaphysics and other sciences complicate the picture.
Yet since ethical problems, practical and theoretical, so commonly and recurrently involve
the distinction in crucial ways, and since
they may be expected to do so even more in the
future, omission of its consideration would
be a serious deficiency.

Without surveying these varieties here or
stipulating a definition, I will explore typical difficulties by using the term in its
popular sense (The way things "really are"
and what is "really best"), trusting the interested reader to detect any variations that
become evident from usage context.

b. Ignorance of the "real." Ignorance is
of many kinds. Each has its own implications
for ethics as a science.

(1) Not know what one already knows. Sometimes a persons forgets. Sometimes a person
errs in calculating. Sometimes persons per-
ceive illusions. Such ignorance, often momentary, seems easily correctable, at least in
principle. Awareness of ignorance normally
begets a feeling of conditional oughtness:
"I ought to improve my memory." "I ought to
be more careful when calculating." "I ought
to try to detect illusions."

(2) Not know what is knowable. More knowledge is commonly available to most persons
than they have appropriated. Whether through
formal education, books, periodicals, other
media, or conversations, more knowledge that
is useful for understanding the way things

are is attainable than most have attained. To
the extent that improvements can come from increased learning, each person "really ought"
to learn more. The problem is social also, so
that group decisions about increasing learning
"really ought" to favor increase, other things
being equal.

(3) Not know what is unknown but knowable
through research. What is not yet known does
not yet enter actual obligations except where
there are possibilities for obtaining knowledge
through research. Then, of course counting the
costs of research and all other things involved,
one ought to engage in research, personal and
social. The importance of scientific research
for obtaining more knowledge about the way
things are becomes greater as we learn more and
use such learning to improve living.

(4) Not know what is unknowable. The "real"
cannot be completely revealed in knowledge. So
partial ignorance of the "real" is a permanent
condition of each person and of mankind. Although one may not know precisely the limits
of knowability, to try to go beyond such limits
seems to be a waste of effort constituting a
conditional "ought not."

c. "Knowledge" of the real uncertain. When
we appeal to scientists for knowledge of the
ways things "really are," we find varying degrees of assurance regarding "hypotheses, theories, and laws," all held with attitudes that
are more or less tentative. So one still cannot be sure about how things "really are" by
consulting scientists. In some areas where
skills have been acquired and used successful-
ly for a long time, as in driving automobiles,
the information obtainable from skilled opera-
tors can be quite reliable. Here, the way
things "really are" and what kinds of actions
and habits are "really best" seem attainable
to common satisfaction. But an expert driver

includes alterness to novelties, to unexpected dangers, and to sudden surprises among his
advice and spontaneous flexibility in responding to them among his ideals.

This problem of uncertainty about our knowledge seems likely to increase because, in
spite of increasing numbers of reliable demon-
strations, we are both discovering more intricate complexities inherent in the nature of
things and creating more intricately complex
social structures and processes that defy clear
comprehension. So, although ethics as a science
should make evident the oughtness to increase
certainty when possible, it should also make
evident that increasing uncertainties also inhere in increasing our knowledge and society.

d. "Knowledge" of the real unreliable.
Some persons earnestly seeking to know the
"real" approach, or are approached by, persons
accepted as authorities in their communities.
When such authorities are fanatical sectarians,
idologists, or deliberate deceivers, false information is taught as true. A person accepting such authoritative teaching has actual
oughts in terms of apparent truths that are
really false. Scientific knowledge is often
misrepresented and misunderstood, both when
hasty generalizations are announced as reliable and when reliable generalizations are interpreted as claiming more than is warranted.
Ethical problems involved in news reporting,
headline writing, and advertizing are well
known.

e. "Knowledge" of the real harmful. Sometimes use of knowledge has unexpected harmful
effects. Before gunpowder and guns where
available, nobody was killed by guns. Now
persons who do not have guns are less likely
to be harmed by them. Today the problem takes
the form of nuclear proliferation and efforts
to prevent availability of nuclear bombs for

terrorist blackmail. So some knowledge that
is useful may also be harmful. Thus any ought
to know what "really is" should be conditioned
by both how it is "really good" and "really bad."
Whenever it is known that knowledge will be, or
may be, harmful, conditional obligations regarding censorship, self-censorship as well as public sensorship, occur.

Since knowledge of what "really is" and of
what is "really best" continues to be conditioned by ignorance of the real, uncertainty about
the real, unreliability of knowledge of the real,
and harmfulness of knowledge of the real, the
proposal that oughtness consists in the power
which the "really greater goood" has over the
"really lesser good" in compelling our choices
creates more problems for ethics than it solves.

f. "Real" must become apparent. Although
whenever faced with a choice between a merely
apparently greater good and a "really greater
good" one should choose the "really greater
good," such "really greater good" must appear
as an alternative for choosing and thus be apparent in the sense intended by our definition.
The issue at stake regarding apparent versus
"real" oughtness has to do, not with whether
or not the one is an apparent alternative and
the other a non-apparent alternative, since
both must be apparent alternatives in any actual
choice, but with the reliability of appearances
in general and of whether, if such reliability
can be improved, an additional kind of ought is
involved. This additional ought is a conditional ought until a person actually chooses to act
in a way intended to improve such reliability.
"Real" oughtness is a conditional oughtness concerned with improving the quality of oughts,
both actual and conditional, if and when possible. It is, in a sense, a kind of ought about
other oughts.[24] Concern here is not so much
with more or less feeling of compulsion but

with more and less confidence in the reliability of knowledge. Epistemological technicali-
ties compounded with knowledge explosion promise
to keep ethics as a science perpetually preoccupied with needs for further clarifications.

2. Implications for ethics as a science.
Complicating the nature of oughtness, including
actual and conditional oughtness, by distin-
quishing between apparent and "real" oughtness
has implications for ethics.

a. Ethics extends to such difficulties. Even
though ethics as a science can be conceived
quite simply as inquiry into the nature of
oughtness, oughtness is of many kinds and so
inquiry into the general nature of oughtness
remains incomplete until it becomes clear how
that general nature retains embodiment in each
of the special and particular kinds of ought.
Problems concerning the relations of appearance
to reality are perpetual. And ethics as a science will be faced with explaining how oughtness, especially conditional oughtness, is involved in each new kind of apparent reality.

b. Ethics has a stake in the availability
of knowledge. Part of the significance of the
distinction between apparent and "real" oughtness is that persons ought to improve their
oughts when possible and that, when ethics as
a science recognizes this ought-to-improve-oughts
as a fact (conditional ought), then ethics as
a science has a vested interest in whatever im-
proves such oughts. Since increase in knowledge
of all kinds that can be useful in making
choices should improve such choices and such
oughts, ethics as a science has a stake in
such increase.

Although ethics as a pure science, as distinguished from an applied science, aims at
understanding the nature of oughtness and formulating true hypotheses about it, it also has
a stake in successful applications. Once a

distinction is made between apparent and "real"
oughtness and ethics as a science is committed
to recognizing benefits from efforts to improve
knowledge of the way things are, it has a vested interest in the expansion of human knowledge
and in the spread of its availability to, and
application by, more and more persons.

    c. New knowledge changes kinds of oughtness.
Even though the general nature of oughtness does
not change, or does not change much, as a consequence of the addition of new kinds of knowledge, when new kinds of knowledge do occur,
new kinds of oughtness emerge to the extent
that new kinds of alternatives and their com-
parable values appear for choosing. A survey
of the numerous kinds of rapid changes occurring these days should reveal many new kinds of
values and obligations inherent in the changed
conditions.

    A glance at only one kind of change, increase
in population, should suggest different kinds of
oughtness relative to growing numbers of people.
To what extent can each person take the welfare
of all other persons in a group into consideration in evaluating his obligations, when the
group has 5 members, 50 members, 500, 5000,
500,000, 5,000,000, 500,000,000 and 5,000,000,
000 members? Problems of impersonality accumu-
late rapidly, and the ethics of impersonal relations, quite apart from institutional factors,
between quantities of persons change of necessity as quantities increase. The techniques
for dealing with extensive and impersonal obligations must be somewhat different. But oughtness involving impersonal relations exists, both
actually and conditionally, although awareness,
complexity, quality, and compulsiveness vary
considerably with persons and societies. But
awareness of the influences of new kinds of
knowledge in determining new kinds of oughtness
is a part of the responsibility of ethics as

a science, as well as of population experts
and world political leaders.

Among the changes new knowledge brings are
the obsolescence of some older kinds of knowledge and of relevant oughts. Cultural lag,
like deleterious personal habits, tends to
keep alive in personal feelings and social
customs kinds of oughts that should have ex-
pired with the arrival of new kinds of knowledge and relevant oughts. The oughtness of
eliminating obsolete oughts is another fact
(conditional ought) recognized by ethics as
a science. Growing knowledge of the accumu-
lation of obsolete oughts in need of extinction is one of the new kinds of knowledge
generating its own kind of oughts.

3. Implications for other sciences. The
distinction between apparent and "real"
oughtness has implications for both the importance of other sciences for ethics and the
importance of ethics for other sciences.

a. Importance of other sciences for ethics.
Not only is ethics a science dependent on other
sciences for providing knowledge of the ways
things "really are" and what is "really best"
regarding them, but the growing importance of
such knowledge ("Post-industrial society,"
some say, will be a knowledge production and
distribution society) make ethics more and
more dependent on them. This growing dependence can be seen as moving in two directions,
toward larger and more complex problems and
toward smaller and more complex problems.

The more intricately interdependent peoples
become through megalopolitan and global living,
the more ethics as a science will depend on
the knowledge provided by experts in megalopolitan and global complexities. The more
specialized, subspecialized and subsubspecial-
ized scientists and technologists become, the
more complex their knowledge becomes, and the

more ethics as a science depends on them. As
pointed out above, each competent specialist
knows what "really is" and what is "really best"
as far as his own specialty is concerned, and
thus is, of necessity, an ethical authority in
his own field. As more specialties develop,
ethics as a science becomes more dependent on
specialists for their specialized knowledge of
being, goodness and oughtness.

b. Importance of ethics for other sciences.
Awareness by scientists that ethics as a science recognizes each specialist as an ethical
authority in his own field should induce added
measures of self-respect, of awareness of significant service, of meaningful purpose, of
motivation, and even of standards for achievement. Awareness of both specialized and general ethical dimensions of specialized work can
give a specialist a feeling of participation in
the ethical welfare of his larger society. Recognition of interdependence of special and
general can motivate some specialists to inquire
into the nature of ethics as a general science
to supplement and make more excellent their
capacities as ethical specialists. Awareness
of the distinction between apparent and "real"
oughtness can contribute to the mutual services
of ethics and other sciences.

WHAT IS RIGHTNESS?

"Acts are right when and because they are
intended to produce the best results for one's
self in the long run."[25] Acts are right when
and because one intends to act as he ought.
Oughtness consists in the power that an apparently greater good has over an apparently lesser good, etc., in compelling our choices. The
foregoing treatment of oughtness has remained
indefinite regarding the question of "whose
good" or "good for whom"? This question has

been postponed until now both because it involves its own host of complex difficulties concerning which much popular confusion exists and because including them previously would have compounded the difficulties in clarifying the nature and kinds of oughtness. Now we tackle the problem of good for whom directly and propose some hypotheses based partly on evidences from several biological, psychological and social sciences.

1. Best for one's self. Problems concerning the nature of self and society, of persons and groups, are of sufficient importance for ethics and of sufficient complexity that separate chapters (two out of six) are devoted to them. Persons and groups interdepend. Each self is essentially social. In formulating a definition of rightness as "intention to produce the best results for one's self in the long run," I have taken into account each self's social nature which is a much more complicated and pervasive constituent of a self's nature than is commonly recognized. Any reader interpreting "best results for one's self" as "selfish" has not read the following chapters and is misinterpreting what is meant. Full treatment of the nature of rightness as involving what is best for one's self must await the following two chapters.

The second chapter, "Social Ethics," concerns what is best for groups. A person acting as an officer responsible for deciding alternatives regarding the welfare of his group then acts, i.e., as a person acting as an officer, rightly when he intends to produce the best results for his group in the long run. Social ethics is treated here as an extension of personal ethics. It is a necessary extension, because all persons are inherently social. But, since it is also true that persons are influenced and molded, not merely by other

persons, but also by groups and cultures,
those who claim that groups exist prior to persons must be heard. My hypothesis is that persons and groups interdepend in many intricately
complex and dynamic (dialectical[26]) ways, but
that the ultimate bases for moral appeals are
the intrinsic values located in persons and
thus that social ethics is more dependent on
personal ethics than personal ethics is on social ethics in at least one way. Group acts are
right when intended to produce the best results
for the group in the long run, the group always
consisting of persons whose best interests in
the long run are at stake in such group decisions and actions.

2. In the long run. Involved in determining
what is best for a self is the question of how
long a self and its values will last. Given
both the uncertainties of sudden death and the
probabilities of average longevity, what is
best for one's self in the long run can be plan-
ned in terms of both such probabilities and uncertainties. Other factors, each with its own
uncertainties and probabilities, include how
much of one's life can be foreseen at any given
time. In cultures where patterns of living and
lifestyles are comparatively fixed, future prospects often appear quite obvious. But in rapidly changing cultures with newly complex and dynamic opportunities, prospects are much more
uncertain. The more interdependent peoples
become, the more each person's life tends to
be influenced by decisions made by others.
Such uncertainties are factors that must be
taken into consideration in formulating scientific hypotheses generalizing about what is
best for a self in the long run.

Many actual oughts are trivial. A smoker
often has to decide whether to take one more
puff from an almost consumed cigarette. "The
long run" for such a choice is very short.

To the extent that the issue of one more puff
is all that occupies a smoker's attention, the
long run terminates when the cigarette is
snuffed out. Life involves numerous relatively isolated enjoyments and sufferings, and some
persons make a policy of living from moment to
moment and from day to day. Both those who are
very poor and depend on others for their care
and those who are rich enough to have whatever
they want may be justified in adopting such a
policy. But most people, I believe, have problems of deciding what is best for themselves
for weeks, months, years and decades as well
as for days, hours and minutes. "The long run"
relative to any choice depends on how long the
run appears while one is choosing. So what is
meant by "the long run" in my proposed definition of the nature of rightness is a variable
capable of endless variety.

Details about these varieties must await
the following chapters, but here I can general-
ize that each problem that a person confronts
embodies its own apparent futurity and that an
act is right when it intends to produce the
best results in the long run of that apparent
futurity. Rightness is relative and variable
when and because the apparently long run is
relative and variable. But such variability
does not prevent us from making observations
and generalizing about what is common to apparent long runs in such varieties. It does
raise another important question about whether
a person spends too much of his time dealing
with trivial problems and shorter runs and not
enough with more important problems and longer
runs. This raises the problems facing an ethicist to a still higher level of complexity and
uncertainty that must await more developed con-
siderations in the following chapters.

<u>3. Intentions.</u> The rightness of acts is
located in a person's intentions. Those who

judge a person's acts producing either good or
bad results for others as right or wrong regardless of the actor's intentions mistake the nature of rightness and wrongness. The bad results of a person's act, when a person intended
to act but did not intend to produce the bad results, are indeed bad; but the act producing
them was not therefore a wrong act. If one extends the language of conditional oughtness to
conditional wrongness, one may make appropriate
judgments of condemnation. But keeping the distinction between conditional and actual wrongness in mind seems to me to be much more difficult than keeping the distinction between actual and conditional oughtness. The problem is
complicated in ethical practice when a person
is unclear about his intentions, regrets or
feels guilty about the consequences, and is con-
demned by those harmed. But so far as ethics
as a science is concerned with basic generalizations about the rightness and wrongness of acts,
rightness and wrongness apply appropriately
primarily to the intentions of the person acting.

I have said that actual oughtness involves
intention and that intention involves at least
volition, what is intended, and degrees, as well
as varieties of modification through a series
of intentions and shared intentions. The topic
is much more complicated and will benefit from
further research. Questions become more intricate as we inquire about how much of a self one
commits when intending and how many and how wide
variations occur in such commitments. When an
action is "wholly intended," does a person com-
mit his whole self in action? His whole future?
His whole will, irrevocably? Are most commitments partial and temporary? Does a self have
many conflicting interests, so that, in most in-
intentions, a self ought to refrain from pre-
judging how future coices will be made in light
of future apparent values?

The problems concerning the nature and kinds
of intention, and thus of rightness and wrongness, will be seen as still more complicated
as we develop further details about the nature
of persons and groups in the following chapters.

Chapter III

PERSONAL ETHICS

If oughtness is the power that an apparently greater good has over an apparently lesser
good in compelling our choices, the question
remains: "Good for whom?" Although some ethical choices may be quite objective in the
sense that the values at stake appear entirely
those of other persons ("Irish Protestants
and Catholics ought to stop fighting each other.") and that many kinds of conditional oughts
are expected to be equally available to many
persons ("When whittling, you ought to keep
the sharp edge turned away from your body."),
I believe that ethics as a science will remain
inadequate until it becomes clear the extent
to which oughtness and rightness have ultimate
foundations in self-interest. I here propose
acceptance of the "wise self-interest" theory
as the truest and best basis on which to build
ethics as a science.

Oughts concerning the interests of others,
oughts concerning the interests of groups and
oughts judged to be objective can be shown to
have the ultimate bases for their appeals in
the oughts that each person understands and
experiences in himself. Other theories that
do have significant relevance to the nature
of oughtness and rightness can be shown to
have foundations in the wise, or enlightened,
self-interest theory.

Given the enlightened self-interest theory
as basic, a primary task of ethics as a science
is to understand the nature of self and the
nature of its interests. This task cannot be
completed here. But an effort will be made to
explore some of the factors essential to understanding the nature of both.

THE NATURE OF SELF

If selfology, the science of self, had been
developed, ethics as a science would appeal
to its conclusions as providing such understanding and to its supply of bases for conditional oughts. But absence of such a science compels ethics as a science to undertake
at least as much exploratory research and
hypotheses about the nature of self and its
interests as are needed for stating and explaining how oughtness both originates in the
nature of self and how all oughtness has its
goal in what is best for self.

I propose that the nature of self can best
be understood as an organic unity, as a whole
of parts, as something both continuingly simple and as increasingly complex, and as something that remains the same in some ways
throughout its lifetime and changes in some
ways from moment to moment, day to day, year
to year, and decade to decade. Simpler minds
may prefer simpler conceptions of self. But
we fail to do justice to the nature of self
unless we recognize both all of the constituent aspects and functions of self as described
for us by numerous sciences and that all do
somehow cooperate in maintaining some personal
integrity throughout life.

A survey of the sciences providing some
understanding of the nature of self seems help-
ful. This sketch of some of the problems and
conclusions from other sciences is far from
complete. But it indicates how ethics as a
science depends on many other sciences for
information necessary for understanding the
nature of self; and ethics as a science needs
not only to appropriate knowledge already
available but also to expect and to encourage
increase in additional knowledge as newer,

sometimes more specialized, sciences develop relevant information.

1. Self as physical. A person's body is a most important part of his self. Each of the physical sciences has something to say about such a body.

a. Physics. A person's body has location in space and time. It has weight, inertia, mass, energy, magnetism, electrical currents in neurones, and brain waves. It is stimulated by light waves in eyes and sound waves in ears and responds sensitively to heat, cold, and atmospheric pressures. It employs principles of leverage and locomotion in its skeletal and muscular systems, and physical principles of pumpling liquids operate in heartbeats and blood circulation.

Not only do these and many other physical principles and processes participate in constituting the human body, but also all of them are essential conditions of its existence and continuation. Consequently each self has a "real" interest in their continuing harmonious cooperation so that it can pursue its other interests. Each essential physical condition that is endangerable may become the basis for a conditional ought. The more a person learns about physics and how physical principles operate in body maintenance, the more conditional oughts he acquires as be becomes aware of possible choices and actions that may endanger his existence or efficient functioning. These oughts are among a self's interests. When dangers seem remote, such interests tend to become dormant, latent, merely potential. But when dangers threaten (collision, explosion, extreme heat or cold, destructive rays), such interests become alive, vital, intense and compelling.

b. Astronomy. Seemingly less revealing of a self's interests, astronomy nevertheless shows

the necessity of galactic, solar and planetary
stability for the evolution and continuance of
life, and how variations in cosmic and solar
radiation influence our weather and other eco-
logical conditions of human survival. Astronomy, by disproving some untenable theologies,
has redirected understanding about the origins,
evolutions, current opportunities and limitations, and future possibilities and prospects
for persons and for mankind. Astronaut moon
landings prepare us for ventures farther into
space, offering hope that some may colonize
other planets before the earth becomes unin-
habitable. Anxious venturers have already
booked high-priced seats on space shuttle
service chartered flights.

Since most persons can do little to influence astronomical processes, their significance
for personal interests may seem slight. Yet
public disturbances about endangering a protective ozone layer in the atmosphere against
cosmic rays, proposals for disposing nuclear
wastes out in space, and fears about falling
satelite debris, serve as evidence of increasing concern, and thus increasing self-interest,
in refraining from actions that may endanger
stronomical conditions essential to living.

  c. Geology and geography. More obvious these
days,when rapid consumption of resources has
made us aware of their limitations and possible
exhaustion, are the values of minerals, petro-
leum, water and fertile soil for human and personal survival. Awareness of progressive pollution of water, air and soil have alerted in
more people self-interest in local, regional,
national and global preservation and repurifi-
cation of these necessities for survival, health
and wealth. Knowing about dangers from earthquakes, volcanic eruptions, drouths, floods,
fires and cyclones provokes awareness of self-
interest in research about their prediction,

prevention and retardation where possible.
Studies in geology and geography have ethical
significance when they reveal the multiplicities
of self-interests each person can have in efficient utilization of natural resources.

Each of the physical sciences and many of
their subsciences can be studied for the purpose of understanding self as physical. The
more fully sciences reveal the physical nature
of things, the more useful they become in en-
abling persons to understand their own interests
as beings both constituted by and surrounded by
physical things and processes upon which their
existence, welfare and happiness depend.

d. Chemistry. The chemical sciences study
molecules, atoms, electrons and other subatomic
particles believed to be the ultimate constituents of physical things. As such, they are constituents of everything both outside and inside
the human body. Everything in a person's envi-
ronment, both animate and inanimate, has chemical constituents, including the earth, air,
water, his clothes, other persons, buildings,
tools, automobiles and food. A healthy body
needs some minimums of proteins, carbohydrates
and fats, and these depend on oxygen, hydrogen,
carbon, sodium, potassium, phosphorus, calcium,
magnesium, iron, iodine, and many other kinds
of atoms. Each chemical needed by a person's
body functions as a source of self-interest
whenever a person becomes aware of the need.
Poisons, allergic substances, vitamins and
hormones, all arouse our interest when we become aware of deficiencies. The nature of self
and of some of its major interests cannot be
fully understood until we appreciate how extensively and intricately pharmacology, that
branch of chemistry specialized to serve human
needs and interests, has developed.

2. Self as biological. Living beings studied
by the biological sciences may seem more closely

related to self-interests since persons more
often identify themselves with such beings.
Not only do selves exist in living bodies,
but characteristics of those bodies play important roles in how persons conceive themselves and, consequently, some of their self-
interests. Hereditary factors, human, racial
and familial, often influence such conceptions
in ways caus: some to be humanists, some
racists and some interest in relatives in their
family tree. The importance that some attribute
to hereditary factors is dramatized today by
controversies over prohibiting or restricting
DNA experiments.

a. Botany. Most people are aware of their
interests in plants, as sources of food and
materials for clothing and shelter. Negative
interests exist also in plants as poisonous,
as sources of allergies, and as weeds. Appreciation of the importance of plants to self
grows when one discovers the crucial role of
chlorophyl in recycling carbon dioxide exhaled
by lungs into inhalable oxygen. Interests in
plants grow also when one discovers the seemingly endless varieties and their variable uses
for medicines and decorations as well as for
foods. The botanical sciences of agriculture,
horticulture and floriculture, for example,
offer opportunities for proliferating a self's
interests.

b. Zoology. The varieties of interests a
self may have in animals include raising them
for food, competing with them as enemies, pet-
ting them as companions, utilizing their labor,
hunting them for sport, and exhibiting them in
zoos. The kinds of animals, quadrupeds, birds,
fish, insects, worms and germs, are so numerous
that study of them continues to be amazing.
Although each person may be interested primarily in those with which he comes in contact,
few persons live without having some animals

significantly influencing their lives. Self-
interest in animals becomes most obvious when
a person is aware of himself as an animal,
having something in common with all other animals, and differing somewhat from all others,
including mammals of the monkey families. Interest in similarities to and differences from other animals takes a special form in medical and
psychological experiments when drugs and learning techniques are tested on other animals first.

    c. <u>Physiology</u>. Human physiology is the bio-
logical science dealing with things with which
persons most frequently identify. The human
body, a marvelous harmony of cells, organs and
systems, has many parts that have a way of calling attention to themselves when deficiencies
occur. Pain sensory end organs pervade the
body. Every pain creates an interest in something that a self naturally seeks to eliminate.
Each system, the circulatory, respiratory, di-
gestive, skeletal, muscular, nervous, glandular,
dermal and reproductive, is complex in itself
and interdepends with all of the others. Each
is essential to life and health. Each grows,
matures and ages, and each has a nature with
typical needs that function as wants constituting self-interests whenever a person becomes
aware of them. Each as a part of the whole
body constitutes a part of what a self as
biological is. Although physiologists have
charted norms and averages, individual differences vary widely in ways that make for many
different kinds of selves.

    How physiological constituents function as
bases for self-interests may be sketched by
listing some of the medical sciences that have
developed to serve those interests: cardiology,
dermatology, gerontology, hematology, immunol-
ogy, neurology, opthalmology, osteology, oto-
larnegology and urology.

3. Self as psychological. Psychology, a
stale joke has it, first lost its psyche or
soul, then its mind, and then consciousness,
leaving it with only the behavior of a body
determined by stimulus-response mechanisms.
When I asked a University of New Mexico col-
league, a psychologist, "What is psychology
today?" he replied: " A branch of biology."
I reject his answer, not as a description of
some prevailing attitudes, but as a description of the task which psychology as a science
has to deal. I do not propose to define psychology as "the science of the self," but
surely problems concerning the nature of self
are among the central problems of psychology
and not something to be pushed to the periphery
or treated as a minor aspect of other problems.
The excuse that self (like psyche, mind and
consciousness) is difficult to measure is un-
acceptable to me. Self, which functions most
actually in self-awareness, self-consciousness,
self-direction and self-criticism, especially
in dialogic interaction with other selves,
is a prime subject for psychological investigation. And it is from psychology that an
ethicist should be able to draw reliable conclusions important for determining the nature
of self, its interests and its oughtness.[1]

Except for physiological psychology, devel-
opmental psychology (genetic, child, adolescent,
aging, etc.) and social psychology, no standard
grouping of the psychological sciences has developed. Much can be learned also from the
many applied fields, including educational
psychology, psychology of counseling, business
psychology, psychology of advertizing, industrial psychology, recreational psychology, psychology of religion, and military psychology.
But these fields also tend to be dominated,
sometimes ruthlessly, by persons indoctrinated
by reductive schools, such as Christian psy-

chology (self as eternal soul), Behavioristic
psychology (J. B. Watson, B. F. Skinner),
Psychoanalysis (S. Freud), and now Existential
psychology. My own view, which I would call
"Organicistic psychology," claims that there is
some truth to each of these schools but that
their reduction of the whole self, and the
whole of psychology, to some important part or
parts constitutes a very clear kind of falsifi-
cation.[2]

Problems facing psychologists include understanding the nature of sensation, perception,
conception, memory, imagination, anticipation,
intuition, inference, reasoning, feelings,
emotions, volition, motivation, preferences,
attitudes, habits, adaptability, personality,
communication, association, and interrelations
of all of the foregoing. Psychologists, like
other scientists, are handicapped by lack of
adequate solution to the mind-body problem.
Thus the interdisciplinary cooperation between
physiologists specializing in the brain and
nervous system and physiological psychologists
experimenting with brain waves is of great importance in overcoming something that handicaps
all sciences.

My primary purpose in the present section
is not criticism of deficiencies but to point
out that each self has potential interests in
each of the problems mentioned above. Sensation, perception, etc., are all essential parts
of a self, and interest in their normal functioning is a natural self-interest. Ethics basic-
ally presupposing enlightened self-interest is
automatically involved in recommending enlightenment regarding the psychological conditions,
processes and principles inherent in the nature
of self. I believe that axiology and ethics as
sciences can be adequate only when they can depend on adequate reliable conclusions by psychologists.

4. Self as sociological. Some of the most
difficult problems in ethics, both in personal practice and in ethics as a science, have
to do with the kinds of oughts each person has
in his relations with others. Especially, in
a society that has idealized individualism,
the obviousness of some kinds of social self-
interests of persons has become shrouded and
even obliterated. But it is especially in revealing the nature of the oughts existing in
persons relative to their associations with
others that ethics as a science can be most
useful in providing a sound basis for policy
decisions, publicly and privately, related
to national interests and the welfare of mankind.

By "self as sociological" I intend to include information about the nature of self as
made available by all of the social sciences.
Limitations of space permit consideration of
only three here. But ethics as a science will
be inadequate to the extent that it omits evidence about the nature of self and its interests and oughts from all of the social sciences, theoretical and applied, including
anthropology, history, jurisprudence and the
administrative sciences.

a. Sociology. Sociology is that general
science inquiring into the nature of groups
and of culture. It includes many more specialized tasks such as inquiring into the natures
of different kinds of groups, of social processes, and especially of the interrelations
of such groups and processes with the nature
and processes in persons.

(1) Social origins of self. The importance
of social interests in constituting the nature
of a self can be seen by recalling social factors essential to its origins.

Although the association of a foetus with
its mother is more intimate than a child

after birth, we interpret association as social only with and after birth. How much self-consciousness and self-development occurs in a foetus is a question needing further research. But the trauma of birth normally assures reactions causing emergence of some self-consciousness, including feelings of volition and agency. Survival of an infant is impossible without feeding and protective care, so an infant is socially dependent whether he is aware of the fact or not. Dependence on maternal milk, bodily warmth and stable, soft, secure holding characterize normal infancy.

The intimacy of nursing mother and child exemplify common interests. Some mothers see their children as still internal parts of themselves become external and so continue to identify themselves with their children. Although an infant is gradually forced to become aware that its mother is a different person, this process is sometimes experienced as traumatic. Awareness of still other persons often occurs as a fearful awakening causing it to cling still tighter to its mother. An infant's self-interest in its caring mother is instinctive. Thus, in a sense, each person's first interests are social.

(2) Self-development as social. Development of self-concepts has two continuing sources, those internal to and those external to the body. A person's feelings of agency, of wanting, of acting are ingredients in self-awareness that vary with feelings of energy, of strength and weakness, of alertness and drowsiness, and of effectiveness and ineffectiveness. The resistance of objects to his actions on them, the painful or pleasing actions of objects on him, and the attitudes of others toward him exemplify external factors influencing self-conception.

The importance of others, their attitudes toward a child, and their actions toward and reactions to a child, in molding conceptions of self has been stressed by George Herbert Mead.[3] Distinguishing between "I" (self as subject or agent) and "me" (self as object or patient), Mead observes that consciousness of "me" occurs as a result of the attitudes and actions that others take towards infants. An infant, like an animal, first acts without attending to himself as a self. He just acts, looks, waves his arms, babbles, without much self-awareness. But when someone looks at him, approaches him, tickles him, picks him up, then he becomes aware of himself as an object of attention, as something looked at, approached, tickled and picked up. By becoming aware of how he reacts to the actions of others toward him, he becomes aware of himself as a reactor. Self-awareness of "me" as an object acted upon thus occurs first, according to Mead, and self-awareness of "I" as the subject which reacts occurs as a result. In this way, conceptions of self, and of self-interest, have social origins.

In another way, as a child grows older, it develops by imitating the behavior of others. A child often integrates his personality by copying the acts of affection, acts of assistance and acts of resistance. "The child by his third or fourth year is a simplified miniature of the mother. If the child is a daughter, she has the same taste in clothes, the same company manners, the same social prejudices, judgments, techniques, virtues and absurdities."[4] Normally a child outgrows his mother model, turns to his father model, to outside models such as the postman, milkman, policeman, bus driver, nurses and teachers. Older brothers and sisters and play group leaders often serve as models. Actual models give way to ideals, some derived from fairy tales, stories of heroes and saints, biography and fiction.

A person's conceptions of his self's interests
thus emerge from many social sources.

Another source of self-development is the
roles each person plays in his groups, family,
play, social and work groups. How a self conceives his interests depends partly on the numbers and kinds of persons, the numbers and kinds
of group functions, and the prevalence of in-
groups and out-groups in which he participates.
When a person becomes identified with an occupation or profession, his own interests tend to
be molded accordingly.[5]

Another important factor in self-conceptions
is the readiness each person has for the role
he plays, since when he does well he is more
proud of himself, feels more secure, serves
with greater confidence, and often produces a
better product. Tragedy often results when a
son, idealizing life as a forest ranger, feels
forced to study medicine to fulfil his father's
ideal that he become a physician. Availability
of skilled occupational counseling can be a
major asset to megalopolitan students. Growth
in awareness of megalopolitan and global opportunities for responsible social roles can make
signficant changes in a self's interests.
Ethics as a science needs to be aware of, and
enable the use of, multiplicities of kinds of
potential interests that can enrich the lives,
the ethical lives, of more persons.

(3) Development of self as social. One may
become aware of how a self depends on social
assistance for the development of its self without becoming aware of how much what is social
is constitutive of the nature of that self.
Each human self is essentially social. The
extents to which, the ways in which, and the
benefits and harms of which, such social factors
constitute each self vary considerably. But
sociologists have observed some nomral minimums
and their importance for wise self-interested

ethical behavior.

Although the examination of the nature and kinds of groups is reserved for the next chapter, Social Ethics, here I must call attention to the importance of primary groups as both an essential, and most efficient, melieux in which a person's initial enlightenment concering his social nature and interests develop naturally. Primary groups are those small (two to sixty), relatively permanent, face-to-face, unspecialized, relatively intimate associations in which persons act confidently as whole persons. Typical "examples of the primary group are the family, or household group, the old-fashioned neighborhood, and the spontaneous play-group of children."[6]

Primary groups are important because they are "the nurseries of human nature." "Human nature is not something existing separately in the individual, but a group nature or primary phase of society. It is the nature which is developed and expressed in those simple face-to-face groups that are somewhat alike in all societies. Man does not have it at birth; he cannot acquire it except through fellowship; and it decays in isolation."[7] Primary groups are important for ethics because in them the end-in-itself, or intrinsic value, character of each self is recognized and presupposed. Each participant becomes aware of his own treatment as an end-in-himself and spontaneously responds by treating others likewise. Each self's awareness of its own intrinsic worth is thus socially established and receives continuing, even if sometimes variable, assurance.

Primary groups are important in many ways. They are efficient humanizers of animal drives. They assure a self's awareness of enduring social respect for his intrinsic value. They mold and habitualize a self's respect for the intrinsic value of others, partly because pri-

mary association is conducive to spontaneously
shared values in which the importance and genu-
ineness of "we-feelings" sometimes surpass those
of I." By participating in a genuine community,
a self not only acquires intuitive understanding of its nature and values but also acquires
and embodies a sharing of such community values
within, or as a part of, himself. When a person identifies himself with a group, he thereby identifies that group with himself.

Another importance of primary groups for
ethics as a science is that the humanizing,
socializing and moralizing services of these
groups is also the foundational source of the
willingness to act morally in other groups.
Secondary groups are more impersonal, often
highly specialized, and capable of serving
only some of each person's interests. Each
kind of group has its own kinds of values, but
most of them depend for the moral understanding
and habits of their members upon their having
acquired them, and in many cases their continuing to reenforce them, in primary group association. As societies become more urbanized, in-
dustrialized, globalized, reduction of time
spent by persons in primary group communion
and communication tends to reduce the readiness
with which each person trusts others to respect
his own intrinsic value and other interests.
Any decline in the power that primary groups
have in providing substantial support for the
moral willingness to serve and be served by
other groups and institutions calls for some
counter measure to resupply awareness of some
ultimate bases for moral appeals needed for
group survival. Decline in primary group association, combined with explosive quantities of
secondary group association, constitutes a pre-
dicament with which ethics as a science must cope.
Any lack in the abilities of ethics as a science to deal effectively with this problem is

a most serious social, political, including national, deficiency.

More specifically, primary groups are sources of our ideals of loyalty, lawfulness and freedom.[8] Those who regret decline in loyalty, lawfulness, and feelings of genuine freedom in our nation would do well to consider their duties and responsibilities for restoring more primary group association. The nature of self as social is conditioned by the number, kinds and qualities of primary, as well as secondary, associations in which it has participated. A person's interests in his groups are among his most fundamental interests. Wise self-interested pursuit of values includes pursuit of those that he has in his groups.

(4) Expansion of self as social. Whenever a person feels benefitted by membership in one group and learns of benefits from membership in another group, then, other things being equal, he is likely to seek membership in still another group. Sometimes a person finds that society has already provided membership for him before he becomes aware of it, as when each child born in a nation is automatically awarded citizenship. Each additional group membership that a person acquires expands his self and its interests through his feeling of identity with that group. In this way, each self acquires additional social interests.

Groups may be divided into two general types through which persons can expand their interests in two different ways. One type tends to be organized geographically, so that larger and larger groups include more territory. A self grows from being mamma's child, to self as a member of a family, self as a play-group member, self as a community member, self as citizen of a county, state, region, continent, and eventually of the world of

mankind. When intimate identification with
one group is conditioned by alienation with
another group, a self tends to acquire relvant
antipathy as one of his self-interests. As a
self expands its identification with persons
in larger groups, it may have to overcome any
feelings of alienation it has acquired for
those groups now included in the larger groups.
Some find value in identification with animals,
either as totems, as pets, or as fellow sentient
beings. Some enjoy feeling identified with their
ancestors, familial, racial, human, and even
animal. Some identify themselves with future
beings, whether biological descendents, pupils
or persons they have influenced, a race, all
mankind, and people, or people-like living
beings, inhabiting other stars of planets.

The other general type of group tends to be
organized for more specialized purposes. Groups
specialzing in producing or supplying services
such as food, clothing, tools, lumber, coal,
gasoline, toys, entertainment, mecical care,
religious ceremony, employment, machine repair,
transportation, education, postal service, insurance, political organization, law enforce-
ment, news and other information, banking,
loans, legal advice, court decisions, etc., all
exist to provide benefits to persons, both
those who are clients served and those who are
employed in serving. Each self served by such
a group has an interest filled thereby. So,
generally speaking, each self that expands its
interests through seeking to serve in and being
served by more specialized groups becomes thereby a more expanded self. Such expansion tends
to involve complexification of self through
acquiring additional interests. Identification
of a self with a specialized group acquires
enormous significance when a person chooses, or
is forced into, a particular occupation or profession. The nature of each person's self-in-

terests thus vary considerably when expanding
through this second general type of group.

Problems, and the ethics of such problems,
involved in expanding self through identification with more and more such groups will be
considered later. Here our task is to become
aware of how extensive, complicated, and variable self-interests can, and often do, become
through different ways of extending self as
social. If each self had unlimited capacity
to expand and complexify, the ethics of self-
interest and self-realization would be comparatively simple. But since each self eventually reaches some limits and since some disvalues normally accompany benefits, awareness
of such limits is also important for each person and for ethics as a science.

(5) Self as cultural. Thus far we have re-
ferred to groups without specific attention
to culture. Culture consists in social habits,
especially those transferred, or at least trans-
ferrable, from person to person, and generation
to generation. Infants are not fully human until they are both socialized and encultured.
Enculturation of an infant begins when a mother
will allow feeding only if it permits itself
to be held in a certain way. Sometimes culture
is imposed on a self, as when a mother corrects
punctuation or spelling. Sometimes culture is
sought avidly by a self, as when one reads
more library books or spends hard-earned money
for college tuition.

Examination of the many kinds, diversities
and complexities of cultures cannot detain us
here. But awareness of the kinds of culture in
which one has been educated, their richness and
usefulness, and of opportunities for acquiring
additional kinds of culture, richer and more
useful, is an important part of a person's understanding of his self. The demonstrated
values of multilingual, muntinational and

multidiscipline achievements need only be mentioned. Persons seeking to maximize values for themselves will not ignore possibilities for expanding self as social through additional cultural achievements when they promise increased cultural riches. A person's self not only has cultural sources but has interests that can be served and satisfied only through cultural means. Some persons experience their greatest enjoyments when believing that they are contributing creatively to enriching culture, whether locally, nationally, or for all mankind.

b. Economics. Persons are economic animals, and their natures and needs tend to be reflected in self-conceptions and self-interests. Each person must eat and thereby consume and destroy some goods. Thus each person is essentially economic in nature. As life becomes intricately more complicated because global production and consumption become more interdependent, the economic nature of many selves becomes increasingly complicated. Ethics as a science must recognize not only each self's essential economic interests but also the increasing complications conditioning the satisfaction of such interests. Interest in respect for skilled workmanship, self-support, efficient productiveness, high quality useful service, economic values that some persons value very highly, needs to be supplemented by interest in inflation rates, fluctuation in foreign exchange rates, trade deficits, deficit spending, world monetary instability, overpopulation, exhaustion of resources, pollution of air, water and land, maldistribution of goods and evils, unemployment, famine, floods, fires, earthquakes and wars.

Economic interests of each self are normally among its most important interests. Some are essential to its life. But despite the truth of claims about the economic determination of history, economic determiners are not the only

determinants of history or of selves. Persons
may seem too self-conscious of their economic
interests when forced to survive through barter
exchange of eggs for potatoes. But the coinage
of money, printing of paper money, checkbook
banking, credit accounting, computerized credit
card purchases, and automatic loans for overdrawn accounts have both facilitated exchange
and stimulated living patterns that make persons virtual slaves to temptations to over-
spending. Some persons believe that, if you
have enough money, you can buy anything. When
so, the importance of obtaining money tends to
become a self's primary interest. Needy persons without money also tend to regard interest
in it as primary.

No simplistic ethics (e.g., reducible to
some ten commandments) can be adequate to account for even economic needs and interests.
Only a very complex science of ethics, one
cognizant of the intricacies of international
finance, multinational corporate management,
and global trade and commerce as well as the
complexities of national industrial conglomer-
ates, federal and state regulations and taxes,
and local adaptations and specialized needs
and productive capacities, to say nothing of
increasing varieties of economic sciences and
subsciences, will suffice to meet current
problems. This is not the place to dwell on
the varieties of interests that a self may
have. But it does seem necessary to call attention to the importance of a self's economic
interests when surveying all of the kinds of
each self normally has.

c. Political science. Each person has political interests essential to his nature,
although awareness of such interests varies
so considerably that some, infants, the ill,
the aged and those completely occupied with
other problems, seem quite oblivious about

such interests and that others, public offi-
cials, political refugees, military personnel,
lawyers, political party officers, persons
wanted by police as lawbreakers, ideological
agitators, delinquent tax payers and persons
dependent on public welfare, seem quite completely preoccupied with them. Thus the ethical importance of a self's political interests
may vary, relative to both the magnitude of
harm and benefit involved and the actual awareness and intensity of concern.

Except for some casual, primary, temporary
and trivial groups, where no need for a system
of social control occurs, most groups require
some kind of recognizable organization on which
members can depend to assure accomplishment of
the purposes of the group. Kinds of systems
of government also vary. Government by a single dominating personal authority is exemplified in some families where the father or the
mother head the household, in a feudal district
where a lord manages extensive landholdings,
in some kingdoms, empires, dictatorships,
military commands, and owner-managed companies.
Government by oligarchies, houses of lords,
boards of directors, and city councils distri-
bute governing responsibilities among a few.
Democratic forms vary, both in the popularity
of the electorate, in the structures and modes
of electing representatives, and in the numbers
and varieties of functions government is called
upon to perform. Implications of these variations for ethics as a science are twofold.
First, given an existing form, what kinds of
oughts, conditional and actual, follow from
its nature? Second, so long as questions about
the suitability of the form of government to
the tasks for which it is responsibile are suggested by evils or deficiencies resulting from
it are raised, inquiry into whether and what
improvements ought to be recommended seems

called for. The task of formulating recommendations for political improvement belongs
to political scientists, but calling attention to evidence regarding ethical implications of both old and proposed improved forms
is a task belonging to ethics as a science.

A persisting issue has to do with what
kinds of interests each person properly pursues privately and what kinds are better pursued publicly. This is an ethical issue as
long as, and because, value variables are at
stake. It recurs in many forms, relative to
privacy of personal business and medical re-
cords, public vs. private ownership of proper-
ty and of the means of production, educational services, religious ceremonies, provision
of common utilities, postal services, and
health and medical services. This is not the
place to suggest ways for settling such issues.
But it is the place to call attention to the
urgent need for developing ethics as a science
extensively enough so that issues such as
these can be settled more soundly on bases
demonstrated to be reliable.

Some political causes of American ethical
deficiencies today[9] include the growth of law-
making, the myriads of laws, and the profusion
of lawyers, many of whom in turn become legislators. Difficulties in getting laws enacted
and enforced, including court adversary trial
methods for testing the laws, create an attitude among lawyers, and many others, that "If
it is legal, then it is ethical." What is
ethical then becomes whatever law is enacted
by whatever means. Unfortunately for this
view, the ethical is both prior to and more
extensive than the legal. That is, persons
proposing legislation and voting for or
against it do so rightly or wrongly depending
on whatever appears best for persons involved
in the group. Ethical problems also follow

from enacted legislation. But the importance
for personal self-interest of having all relevant values examined and evaluated wisely prior
to legislation is something that ethics as a
science continues to recognize.

Questions about political rights, duties and
privileges are among those obviously having
ethical implications. Questions about justice
and injustice, distributive and retributive,
are as central to ethics as to political science. Ideals of equality, proclaimed especially by those believing that they are being treated unfairly, can be wrongly overlooked or press-
ed to absurd extremes. All members of a group
are alike in some fundamental respects, and
treatment of all alike in those respects is
probably likely to bring the best results for
the group and its members in the long run. But
each member of a group is also different from
all others in some respects. He may be unique
in some respects. Does each person have an
equal right to have his uniqueness, and his
differences from others, also respected? If so,
then does it follow that the best policy is
one that treats all persons alike in whatever
ways they are alike, and differently, i.e.,
equally differently, in whatever ways they are
different? I do not wish to settle this question here, but its settlement as a general ethical principle seems an appropriate task for
ethics as a science. Much disagreement about
political rights and duties results in part
from failure to have this question settled as
a fundamental ethical principle.

I must resist raising other questions here
about the numerous kinds of political issues
that have important relevance for each self's
interests. Awareness of the fact that each
person lives in a whole hierarchy of groups,
each group at each level having its own problems that have bearings on personal welfare,

and that absence of a minimum effective world
government seriously jeopardizes each person's
prospects for survival and welfare, should motivate more persons to help establish ethics
as a science devoted to understanding and improving the reliability of ethical principles
needed for sounder guidance of the vast multi-
plicity of political groups.

5. Self as organic. The foregoing listing
of contributions of numerous sciences to understanding the nature of self and its interests
leaves a mistaken conception of plurality without unity that needs correction. Emphasis in
the foregoing has been upon the multiplicities
and varieties that a self may or must acquire.
I do not wish to detract from such list of
multiplicities because many more possibilities
have been neglected. But there is another side
to each self, and that is its integrity, unity,
persistence and substantiality.

Questions about how a self, or anything, can
be both a whole and parts plague those who view
wholes and parts as opposites, especially as
contradictory opposites. Of many false views,
I mention only three, all seemingly popular.
Those emphasizing self as a whole have sometimes sterilized it of parts, conceiving it
as a simple soul, eternal in nature and thus
unaffected or only superficially affected by
time. Those emphasizing self as parts have
sometimes denied it any wholeness, claiming
either that it consists entirely of some ultimate particles, whether material particles or
quanta of energy, or that it exists only momen-
tarily, serially recurring in successive moments of consciousness. Those claiming that
a self includes both soul and body, the one
existing as an indivisible whole and the other
existing as inherently subdivided parts tempo-
rarily existing together, involve unresolvable
paradoxes when trying to explain mind-body

problems.[10] The prevalence of these false
views is a great handicap to ethics as a science
because they prevent clear and adequate conceptions of how all of the multiplicities of parts,
i.e., the varieties of self-interest outlined
above, contribute more or less harmoniously to
the substantial unity of each self as a whole.

An enlightened self-interest theory of ethics
can be recommended only when accompanied by an
enlightened conception of self and enlightened
conceptions of a self's interests. The importance of utilizing scientific methods in formulating and refining truer and more realistic
conceptions of self and in drawing on conclusions already available from many established
sciences can hardly be underestimated.

A fully adequate theory of the nature of self
cannot be developed here. But the observation
that the whole and parts of a self are complementary, not contradictory, can be made with
confidence. When a whole is conceived as not
its parts and its parts are conceived as not its
whole, then a self conceived as inclusive of
both such whole and parts exists as a larger,
more complex, more dynamic whole, here called
an organic whole. An organic whole is one incorporating both a whole as opposed to its parts
and parts as opposed to a whole and their complementary oppositions to each other in a larger
harmony.[11] I see one task of ethics as a science
assuming as a basic principle of enlightened
self-interest the further exploration of how
the complementarily opposed kinds of self-interest can be more efficiently harmonized, more
systematically organized, and more powerfully
integrated.

THE NATURE OF INTERESTS

Depicting self-interest in terms of the multiplicities of interests surveyed above cooperating

more or less harmoniously in serving the interests of a self as a whole leaves many questions about the nature of interests still un-
answered. Some of these questions that must
be dealt with by ethics as a science include
the following.

1. Interests in value. In surveying the
varieties of interests that may constitute a
self's interests, I have presumed that every
interest which a self has involves an interest
in value, positive or negative, good or bad.
The ultimate source of values and other problems concerned with understanding values have
been explored in Axiology: The Science of Values. especially Chapter III, "The Nature of
Values," and will not be restated here. How
intrinsic values are experienced, usually intermingled with conceptions of the natures of
things and the nature of self, is a complicated problem, still not fully understood. But
for practical purposes in dealing with ethical
problems it is convenient to speak of interests
in values as wants, connoting both wanting, including lacking, by a person and something
wanted, and not yet actualized by that person.

Interests have objects or objectives to be
obtained, maintained, or completed and terminated. Such objects are interpreted as, or intended as, having or being value, instrumental
or intrinsic or both. The purpose of ethical
action, i.e., of choosing and acting as one
ought, is to further the obtaining, maintaining or completion of such value. So a self
is by nature a valuing and value-seeking being;
and each good obtained, maintained or completed tends to be seen somehow as increasing
or adding too the goodness of, or the goods
owned by, that self. A good-seeking self
seeks to add good to itself, and this involves
a process of identification of self with whatever is added to it. When evil is in prospect,

a self seeks to avoid or eliminate it, and to obtain or maintain its elimination. When possible, a self seeks to differentiate itself from such evil, and to alienate such evil from itself. Since options regarding goods and evils often involve mixtures and degrees, a self by nature has interest in maximizing goods and minimizing evils.

2. Interests as values. Part of the task of ethics as a science in understanding the nature of self and its interests is that, in addition to concern about interests in values, where attention is focused on objects or objectives as better or worse, concern about the values of having or not having interests, about having too few or too many interests, about whether some interests are better than others is needed. That is, understanding the natures and values of interests is as important as, perhaps more important than, understanding the nature of interests as interests in values. Concern about values of interests encounters many problems.

a. Values of having interests. Although a person can hardly be alive without having some interests, observing that persons lacking in motivation enjoy life less begets questions about the values of having interests. Most persons experience apathy as valueless or as having negative value. Life cannot be interesting unless one has interests. So having at least some interests seems better than having none.

However, an opposing view needs consideration. Many Hindus hold that desire is the source of all genuine evil, since desire leads to frustration, and both desire and frustration keep a naturally quiescent self agitated rather than peaceful. They conclude that one ought to try to eliminate all desires and interests. Having no interests is better than having some,

according to this view. Although I do not
hold this Hindu view, I do believe that ethics
as a science ought to examine all kinds of
evidence related to the values of having
interests.

b. Values of kinds of interests. Are some
kinds of interests better than others? Some
interests are momentary, others more lasting.
Some interests are more intense, others more
calm. Some interests are simpler, others more
complex. Some interests are rigid, others
more flexible. Some interests are more active,
others more passive. Some interests are more
creative, others more destructive or consumptive. If it can be determined that some kinds
of interests are better than others, either as
interests regardless of what they are interests
in or as interests causing differences in what
they are interests in, then ethics as a science
should seek to discover any stable bases for
conditional oughts regarding such kinds.

c. Values of more or less interests. Can a
person have too many interests? When a person
has more active and actual interests than he
can serve, he becomes frustrated. Frustration
is experienced as an evil. When a person suffers frustration because he has too many interests than he can satisfy, does he not have
too many interests?

Can a person have too few interests? Even
a person sufficiently motivated to have escaped
apathy and laziness may still be at a loss as
to what to do. Rural environments sometimes
fail to provide stimuli to enough interests
to keep vigorous youths enjoyably occupied.
Active children with very restricted opportunities often respond with rage. Ethics as a
science should include research regarding possible principles relative to persons having
too many or too few interests.

d. Values of more or less kinds of interests.

A person may have many, even too many, interests
of one kind but not have interests of enough
kinds. Whether or not the words "narrow-minded"
and "broad-minded" are appropriate here, persons
experiencing first a few kinds and then many
kinds often testify to enriched opportunities
for enjoyment and self-realization. If so, then
ethics as a science should investigate whether
any reliable bases for conditional oughts exist
relative to having more kinds of values.

Persons with simpler abilities, whether under-
developed children or incapacitated persons or
the aged with declining energies, may be happier
if not pressured into having interests beyond
their capacities to fulfill. Although some developments have occurred regarding understanding
problems of the aged, gerontology is still in
its infancy. Understanding the oughtness of
reducing the numbers of kinds of interests by
persons during their "declining years" is another task for ethics as a science.

e. Intrinsic values of interests. Interests
usually have both instrumental and intrinsic
values. As instrumental, they motivate action
to achieve satisfaction or to suffer frustration. As instrumental, they contribute to the
occurrence of other values. As intrinsic, they
are experienced as enjoyed or suffered. If one
enjoys an interest when it is more complex, more
persistent or more intense, then such enjoyment
is experienced as more intrinsic goodness. Those
interests enjoyed as greater intrinsic goodness
are intrinsically better than those enjoyed as
less.

The task of understanding how much attention
a person ought to give to the intrinsic values
of his interests as compared with their instrumental values and other resulting intrinsic values is available for suitable research. Persons differ, but in a time when policy deciders
are worried about the exhaustion of resources

116

the possibilities regarding increased benefits
that may result from maximizing enjoyment of
interests themselves as intrinsic values should
be exploited.

f. Interdependence of interests and objects.
Some objects are more interesting than others,
and thus arouse more interests. Some interests
are more variable than others and thus can lead
to interests in more objects. Sometimes objects
seem to have more influence in arousing interests
and sometimes interests have more influence in
locating objects of interest. Interests and
objects not only interdepend but influence each
other variably.

Furthermore, we can observe that selves sometimes have enduring interests in momentary objects, sometimes momentary interests in enduring
objects, sometimes enduring interests in enduring objects, and sometimes momentary interests
in momentary objects. Further study of questions regarding the varieties of interrelations
and interdependencies of interests and objects
may provide further enlightenment useful for
an ethics of enlightened self-interest.

3. Apparent and real interests. In the foregoing I have neglected to distinguish between
"apparent" and "real" interests. Now problems
both in distinguishing between apparent and real
interests and the importance of such a distinction and its implications for enlightened
self-interested ethics must be faced.

Problems involved in distinguishing between
the apparent and real have plagued us before
and will continue to plague us as persons and
ethics as a science. The problem of apparent
and real values was dealt with in Axiology:
The Science of Values, pp. 88-91 and 119-127.
The problem of apparent and real oughtness
was dealt with in the previous chapter, pp.
pp. 73-81. Now we must examine problems involved in distinguishing between an apparent

and real self and its apparent and real interests.

Each self appears to itself in some way most
of its waking (and much of its sleeping and
dreaming) time. Each person has some conception
or, more likely, several conceptions of his self.
Persons have attitudes toward themselves of lik-
ing and disliking, approving and disapproving,
that vary with circumstances. Some persons are
much more self-reflective than others, and they
spend much more time thinking about themselves.
Persons differ regarding what they think most
about when self-reflecting; some are concerned
with facial beauty and skin care, some about
temptations to dishonesty endangering integrity,
some about themselves as owners of wealth, re-
putation, social position or achievement. Some
are concerned about their digestion, their
physique, their stamina, their aggressiveness,
their healthiness and resistance to disease.
Some are concerned about what people will, or
do, think of them. Some seem so preoccupied
with other things that they remain largely
unselfconscious. Thus preoccupations with
self-awareness vary.

Despite variations, from person to person
and within each person, the way a self appears
to itself largely determines what it will conceive to be its primary interests. Although
a person's interests, and oughts when he chooses
between interests, are naturally conceived in
terms of how he conceives himself, he normally
faces questions from time to time about whether
or not he should have better interests. When
a person pursues two interests, one of which
gives him more enjoyment than the other, then,
other things being equal, he ought to pursue
the more enjoyable one more. People normally
do as they ought, or try to do as they ought,
when things so appear.

When a person becomes aware that he has more

interests than appear to him at that time, he
thereby recognizes that he has some "real"
interests. If by "real" we mean "exist whether
or not they appear," then all of a person's
interests of which he is not now aware are his
"real" interests in this sense of the term.
Some of these were apparent to him moments ago.
Some are familiar to him but he has not thought
about them for several days. Some have occurred to him once in the past, but he has forgot-
ten about them. Some, if we extend the notion
of interests to potential interests, are known
about by scientists, but he has not yet learned about them. Some not even scientists know
about. Thus the word "real" in this sense includes a whole range of interests from those
of which he is now aware to those potential
interests a person would have if he know what
scientists know about his nature and even what
scientists do not yet know.

When a person becomes better acquainted
with more of his potential interests and has
more of his interests in mind, then he should
be able to make better choices because he then
takes more values into consideration. So one
problem facing persons, and ethics as a science, is to try to increase acquaintance with
potential interests and to have more of them
in mind when making choices. Although actual
oughts exist only when a person faced with
choices between alternative apparent interests,
real interests can enter actual oughts whenever
they become apparent. Some interests are merely apparent, as when one, in a dream, desires
another cup of coffee. Some interests are apparently real, as when he learns from his physician that he has a cancer.

Questions about the real nature of things,
which are properly investigated by various
sciences, have ethical significance whenever
knowledge about such things may improve the

welfare and happiness, to say nothing about
chances for survival, of persons. Oftentimes
what a person has yet to learn about the natures of things that do or may affect his welfare is much greater than what he has already
learned. This is especially true for children.
When a person becomes aware of the values of
such learning, he acquires some oughts, both
actual and conditional, about such learning.
Since a person naturally most wants what is
best for himself, when he recognizes that
oughtness consists in choosing and doing what
is best for himself, then he realizes that he
most wants to do what he ought to do, because
what he ought to do is what he most wants to
do. The most difficult problems facing persons are not whether or not to do what one
ought to do, but to discover what is really
best for one's self in the long run.

Many of the interests surveyed above (studied
by physical, biological, psychological and
social sciences) are "real" interests of which
many persons are not familiar. Thus, although
"real" in our present sense because potential,
they are not actual interests of those persons
because those persons are not aware of them.
One kind of difficulty that some find with the
theory and practice of self-interest is that
actual oughtness always exists in terms of
actual interests, whereas, once we learn more
about the natures and values of things, actual
oughtness often compels a different course of
action than before. Others find opportunities
for growth in knowledge not so much a difficulty
as a value, and acquire feelings of actual oughtness for increasing their knowledge. For them,
pursuit of scientific knowledge becomes a primary interest and a constantly recurring actual
ought.

4. Kinds of interests. Although the foregoing survey of sciences was a kind of survey
of kinds of interests, interests may be classified in many other ways all relevant to understanding the nature of a self and its interests
and all having significance for ethical choices.
The following list of kinds is far from complete. But it should suggest kinds of factors
that need serious, and sometimes constant, consideration in ethics as a science.

a. Essential versus non-essential. Whatever
is essential to life and survival is automatically of interest to persons. Among each of the
groups of sciences surveyed above, some essen-
tials of life were mentioned. Where interests
in what is essential to maintain life are concerned, we can infer as a conditional ought,
other things being equal, that one ought always
have such interests. I will not suggest such
a list here, but surely ethics as a science
should prepare such a list with the help of
all relevant sciences. Whatever is essential
for happiness or whatever is the best goal for
human beings should also automatically be of
interest to persons. I will not suggest such
a list here, but again ethics as a science
should accept as a task the preparation of
such a list. Allowances must be made for varying personality types, cultural backgrounds,
environmental opportunities and individual
capacities. But any reliable list of essenti-
als for living and any reliable list of essen-
tials for happiness common to all mankind
should become available through the services
of ethics as a science and become lists of conditional oughts for every self-interested
person, other things being equal.[12]

b. Important versus trivial. Some interests,
though enjoyable, have little or no value consequences. Other interests influence the course
of one's whole life with many consequences for

happiness or unhappiness. An automobile
driver interested in lighting a cigarette
rightly reaches for his lighter. But when
suddenly dangerous conditions demand his full
attention, then he ought to attend to driving
and forget his interest in lighting a cigarette.

c. Long-range versus short-range. Some interests aim at immediate benefits, others at
long-run benefits. Some interests are long-
range interests because they remain interests
for a long time. Short-run interests include
those we lose quickly, those we consummate
completely, and those we outgrow. Although
some short-range interests may have essential
importance and some long-range interests may
be trivial, long-range interests seem oftener
aimed at larger values and observations suggest
that they more often yield greater benefits.

d. More versus less anticipatory interests.
Some desires are easily, or at least quickly,
satisfied. One does not have to wait long for
satisfaction to be complete. But some interests not only persist but continue to be interests while one works toward their goals. A person can take satisfaction on completing each
step, and can enjoy repeated imaginings of what
the final satisfaction will be like. Robert
Louis Stevenson wrote: "To travel hopefully is
better than to arrive." Some prolonged court-
ships are reported as more enjoyed than consequent marriages.

e. Recurring versus repeatable interests.
Interests in eating, sleeping, excreting, exer-
cising and resting recur naturally. Interests
in going to work daily, week-end parties, paying
bills monthly, celebrating birthdays and holi-
days recur artificially. Other interests in a
unique accident, a highschool beauty contest,
and the death of one's mother are usually unrepeatable. Each kind of interest has its own
values and disvalues.

f. Habitual versus flexible interests.
Habits are adaptations to efficient solution
to similar problems. Habits are repeated responses to problematic situations that produce benefits or reduce harm or both. Whenever the same problems recur, having habits
for successful solution results in efficiency
benefits. However, using habits to respond
to different situations often results in mal-
adaptation and creates rather than solves
problems. Flexible interests aid in survival
and adaptation in relatively new situations.

Awareness of the nature of habits and of
flexibilities and their benefits and dangers
tends to beget interest in them. That is, in
addition to having habitual and flexible interests, one can, and doubtless at times should,
develop interests in having habits and in having flexibility. A self's character is shaped
by the habitual and flexible tendencies that
he develops. Earlier ethicists spoke of habits
(both stable habits and habits of flexibility)
as virtues when they enabled a person to maximize his self-interests wisely.

g. Complex versus simple interests. These
two kinds really involve several kinds since
there are many different kinds of complexities
of interests and of interest complexes. Some
interests tend to create more interests. Some
interests help to satisfy more other interests.
Some interests are satisfiable only through
satisfying others. Some interests give support to a whole hierarchy of interests. Some
interest complexes generate higher-quality
interests.

h. Harmonizing versus disharmonizing interests. A self, aware of having conflicting
interests, tends to develop an interest in
harmonizing all or most other interests in
ways that reduce conflicts among them. Some
interests tend to be sufficiently self-propel-

ling and self-sustaining that they dominate
attention and effort at the expense of other
equally important or even more important interests. Manias and phobies sometimes conflict
with other beneficial interests in ways detrimental to their development and satisfaction.
    i. Interest in optimizing interests. In ad-
dition to interests of many kinds, interest in
growth of interests, interest in habitual and
flexible interests, and interest in harmonizing
interests is the interest in maximizing the
values of one's life as a whole. Maximizing
means producing the most good with the least
evil possible. When recognizing possibilities
of both too much and too little, and that the
maximum possible may be too much, then this
same interest in maximizing becomes an interest
in optimizing, for by most possible we really
mean the best possible.
    This interest often involves an interest
in planning one's other interests so that such
optimum becomes possible. This interest is opposed by disinterest in planning, exemplified
by those who live a day at a time, meet their
problems as they come, and muddle through as
fate, luck and circumstances permit. Disinterest in planning is supported by Zen, which
plans not to plan for tomorrow. But "care not
for the morrow" plans require more trust in
nature's providence than megalopolitan society
can provide, unless ample welfare programs supplement nature's providence sufficiently. Interest in optimizing interests is one kind of
interest that every intelligent person has.
    5. Can interests be rated? Are some inter-
ests better than others? Are some kinds of interests better than others? Yes. Those that
result in more enjoyment and/or less suffering.
Although the problem of rating is, as personal,
something that must await further developments
of ethics as a research science, I can suggest

the following principles as hypothese for further consideration by those dealing with this
question. The paragraph-heading letters refer
also to the kinds of interests outlined in the
previous section.

a. Essential versus non-essential. When
faced with a choice between pursuing an interest in something essential to life and pursuing
one in something not essential to life, one
ought always choose the former, other things
being equal. And when faced with a choice between pursuing an interest in something essential to happiness and in pursuing an interest
in something not essential to happiness, one
ought always choose the former, other things
being equal.

b. Important versus trivial. When faced
with a choice between pursuing an interest in
something that is important and pursuing an
interest in something that is trivial, one
ought always choose the former, other things
being equal.

c. Long-range verus short-range. When
faced with a choice between pursuing a long-
range interest and pursuing a short-range interest, one ought always choose the former,
other things being equal.

d. More versus less anticipatory interests.
When faced with a choice between pursuing an
interest with more anticipatory satisfactions
and one with fewer anticipatory satisfactions,
one ought always to choose the former, other
things being equal.

e. Recurring vs. unrepeatable interests.
No principle recommended.

f. Habitual versus flexible interests.
When faced with a choice between developing a
habit for solving recurrent problems and not
developing such a habit, one ought always
choose the former, other things being equal.
When faced with the choice between developing

capacity for flexibility in dealing with new
problems and not developing such flexibility,
one ought always choose the former, other
things being equal.

g. Complex versus simple interests. When
faced with a choice between pursuing a complex
interest serving and being served by many other
interests and a simple interest, one ought
always choose the former, other things being
equal.

h. Harmonizing versus disharmonizing interests. When faced with a choice of pursuing a
harmonizing interest and pursuing a disharmonizing interest, one ought always choose the
former, other things being equal.

i. Interest in optimizing interests. When
faced with a choice of pursuing an interest in
optimizing interests and pursuing an interest
that does not optimize interests, one ought
always choose the former, other things being
equal.

6. Conflicts of interests. Self-interest is
plagued by conflicts such that satisfaction of
some interests prevents satisfaction of others.
Although persons with fewer and simpler interests tend to suffer less from such conflicts,
all do suffer. Since more, and more complex,
interests proliferate as life becomes more
megalopolitan and global, more conflicts and
more complicated conflicts can be expected.
Some of each person's conflicts of interests
result from his group memberships and conflicts
within and between such groups. So as life becomes more complicated, each person's interests
can be expected to incorporate more conflicts
from such sources.

a. Why occur? Why do conflicts of interests
occur? Because a person acquires too many interests, i.e., more than can be satisfied at
any one time and perhaps even during all of
his time. Each person naturally acquires more

and more interests as he becomes acquainted
with more and more things, persons and groups,
as well as better acquainted with his own real
self. Cultural factors stimulating his interests, including family examples, educational
systems, communications media availability and
interestingness, contacts with more people,
occupational training and service demands, and
self-motivation when persons acquire habits of
curiosity and intellectual exploration. Opportunities for travel, ownership of more kinds
and more complicated instruments, and stimuli
from profitable advertizing and salesmanship
promote proliferation of interests.

   b. Conflicts as evils. When conflicts between interests cause frustration of some interests and when such frustrations are experienced as evils, such conflicts are judged to
be evils. When goods desired are not obtained,
awareness of such lack is experienced as evil.
When this is so, then the more conflicts of
interests that occur the greater the number of
evils that result. The evils are especially
great when interests essential to life or essential to health or happiness are drawn into
such conflicts. Evils appear especially se-
vere when persons pursue them with intimate
involvement and intense desire and expecta-
tion. The evils often seem more annoying
when more frequently recurring. To the extent that conflicts of interests are evils,
effort ought to be made to eliminate or reduce them as much as possible. A major function of ethics as a science is to understand
the nature of interests and their conflicts
and ways to reduce the evils of such conflicts
as much as possible.

   c. Benefits from conflicts. Pursuit of interests requiring bodily energy consumption
and consumption of time, money and other resources involve costs which, when excessive,

become evils. When conflict of interests results in eliminating some resource-consuming
interests, the results may be seen as good.

Body and mind both tend to degenerage when
not exercized sufficiently. When a person no
longer has to choose, because all of his desires
are being satisfied, his problem-solving ability,
and his ethical sensitivity, tend to diminish.
Persons continuingly practicing choosing (exemplified by some parents of young children and
some administrators plagued with a plethora of
policy decisions) tend to develop great ethical
sensitivity, more understanding of value issues
and of how to resolve them, and increased intelligence in problem solving. When this occurs,
it may be seen as one benefit of having conflicts
of interests.

Ethics originates in and continues to depend
on conflicts of interests for its existence and
nature. Oughts exist because persons are faced
with choices between alternatives not both of
which can be attained. Only because conflicts
of interests exist, i.e., interest in two or
more alternatives not both of which can be attained, does oughtness, and thus ethics, exist.
It may be that life would be better if there
were no ethics, oughtness or choices. But no
heavens, kaivalya or utopias have yet been
established on earth. Any benefits derivable
from ethics owe their existence to the existence
of conflicts of interests.

Since many interests in additional social
and cultural riches can be attained only with
conflicts of interest inherent in them and between them, additional conflicts are a price
that must be paid by persons seeking and acquiring such additional riches. Although the
conflicts themselves do not seem beneficial,
if they are part of the cost of acquiring richer, more-complicated, higher-quality, and more-
enduring satisfactions, then the greater bene-

128

fits of such acquisitions may so much outweigh
their evils that they are often easily included as part of a much-preferred alternative in
wise choosing.

    <u>7. Can conflicts be reduced?</u> Yes. There
are ways to reduce some conflicts, and there
are ways to reduce the evils of some conflicts.
Discovering these ways is a task inherent in
the nature of ethics as a science and of wise
self-interest, which we next examine more
more closely.

WISE SELF-INTEREST

    Althought each person naturally wants what
is best for himself and naturally tries to
choose and to do what is best for himself (i.e.,
to choose and do what he ought to do), somehow
he fails part of the time. Each person seems
to himself to acquire some evils that he does
not want and less than the best and less than
all of what he wants. When this happens, he
also naturally wonders whether he did all that
he ought to have done and what he ought to do
now to overcome unwanted evils and deficiencies
in the quality and quantity of goods he wants.
    The general answer to his question, accord-
ing to the enlightened self-interest theory
being proposed here, is to seek more enlightenment. No person fully understands the nature
of his self and its interests. No person fully
understands the nature of the world which both
enables him to live and to satisfy some interests and prevents him from living forever and
from satisfying all of his interests. When a
person learns enough about the nature of his
self, its values, its interests, and the world
and its availability and unavailability as a
means for serving his needs and wants, then he
should be able to choose and to act more wisely.
That is, by achieving sufficient enlightenment

about the nature of existence and values and
how best to attain what he wants, one will be
enabled to choose more wisely. He should know
how to attain and enjoy more of what he wants
when he wants what is really best for himself
in the long run.

The theory of enlightened self-interest advocates achieving more enlightenment so as to
increase optimization of values, and then acting accordingly. The theory of wise self-interest advocates achieving sufficient such enlightenment to actually enjoy life and optimized values, and acting accordingly. No person is wise
until he is happy. Wise self-interest behavior
is an ideal that the enlightened seek to realize.
Englightened self-interested persons keep seeking to improve their abilities to achieve happiness.

Suggestions about how to improve abilities
for improving probabilities for wise self-interested self-realization will include suggestions about (1) self-development, (2) interpersonal development, (3) social development,
(4) relations with the rest-of-the-world development, and (5) development of one's life as a
whole.

1. Wise self-development. The more fully a
person understands his own self, the better he
should be able to choose wisely. As such understanding increases, he still faces some typical
problems.

a. Choose the best interests. Which of a
person's too many interests ought he seek to
realize? Although individual peculiarities must
be taken into account, some insights as to which
interests are best to develop can be gained from
studying each of the relevant sciences. These
sciences usually aim to understand both any universal traits common to all persons and traits
common to different kinds of persons in ways
that suggest what is better or worse for one's

self. Some principles for choosing among interests were suggested above when "Can principles be rated?" was discussed.

Although one ought always to choose essential in preference to non-essential interests, other things being equal, it is also true that non-essential interests may constitute most of one's interests and, surely, having some non-essential interests is itself essential to life, for all except those whose lives are in extreme danger. Although longe-range interests are preferable to short-range interests, other things being equal, most of one's interests are short-range. Part of the reason for long-range interests is that they enable pursuit of more short-range interests later. Although harmonizing interests are preferable to disharmonizing interests, other things being equal, some interests of the moment can be so enjoyable as to be landmarks in memory despite their disharmonizing effects. Selecting the best interests may include some of both important and trivial, recurring and unrepeatable, habitual and flexible, complex and simple, as well as essential and non-essential and long-range and short-range.

b. Reduce conflicts between interests. Since much unhappiness results from recurrent frustrations, elimination when possible of those interests causing such frustrations is desirable. When frustrations result from having too many interests, reduction of the number of interests seems wise. When pursuit of one interest causes frustrations relative to many other interests, perhaps it should be eliminated, unless of course it is more important for survival and happiness. Sometimes depth psychology can aid in identifying interests with different levels within a personality, so that conflicts will be suffered less when located at a surface level and integrity and stability can be enjoyed at deeper levels. Conceiving some sufferings as subordinate parts of larger systemic achievements tends to reduce or modify them somewhat, as when muscle aches from exercize are understood as instrumental to keeping fit. Conceiving conflicts in terms of complementary instead of contradictory opposites reduces the apparent sharpness of some conflicts.

One psychological principle, discovered and stated in ancient times, which continues to be obvious to all once it is clearly understood, is that "desire for what will not be obtained ends in frustration; therefore, to avoid frustration, avoid desiring what will not be attained." This principle was stated so effectively and convincingly that it gained its formulater first the honorific title of "The Englightened One," i.e., The Buddha, and later virtual deification.[13] The principle involves a willingness to accept things as they come, and is reflected in an attitude and way of living called Zen.[14] It involves a willingness to be frustrated as much as one is frustrated and a willingness to be as ambitious as one is ambitious and a willingness to do as one ought in whatever way such oughtness appears. The principle is an hypothsis researchable by scientific methods. But once the principle is clearly understood, any research proposal will seem superfluous.

c. Best balance of interests. Pursuit and some satisfactory achievement of all of several kinds of interests is essential to survival and happiness. When undue attention, time, effort and resources are devoted to some or even one at the expense of others equally essential, then such imbalance of attention to one's own interests causes suffering. Although the ideal of a well-rounded person prevalent during the Twenties had to give way as impossible of realization due to knowledge explosion and increasing difficulties of expanded mastery, nevertheless interest in personal integrity requires

some minimum degree of balance among one's
basic interests. How to achieve and maintain
such minimum becomes increasingly difficult
as the requirements of special-interest-group
memberships, including those of occupational
and professional groups, become more demanding.
The tendency of many to settle for the ideal
of a "well-rounded specialist," with its built-
in deficiencies, is one to which many succumb.[15]
No pattern of balances can be preplanned for
all. But that each person should achieve some
minimum balance does seem essential to wise
self-interested development.

One principle regarding a best balance of
interests is the standard one of avoiding reductionism whenever possible. Reducationism
is the tendency, and the philosophy approving
the tendency, to accept some part of a whole
as if it were the whole, or as the most essential part of the whole, so that choices regarding all other parts are rendered subservi-
ent to those favoring the the over-emphasized
part. Pressures from special-interest groups,
whether religious sects, racist groups, specialized occupations and professions, societies
of specialized scientists, or economic or social classes, all tend to emphasize their specialized interests. The tendency to overemphasis,
and thus to reductionism, is often irresistible.
Reductionism is a natural enemy of wise self-
realization through balance of interests. Difficulties of achieving balance may become more
obvious as we explore the following suggestions
for improving abilities.

2. Wise interpersonal development. Selfishness is the chief enemy of wise self-interest.
Persons who are selfish sooner or later, usually sooner, often immediately, suffer from their
selfishness. Although I propose the foregoing
statements as hypotheses for appropriate testing, the evidence available to me suggests that

they will be confirmed as general principles
of interpersonal interaction. The reasons why
selfishness is inimical to self-interest can
be induced by observing people interacting.

The most important principle to observe is
the principle of reciprocity. People have a
tendency to treat others as they are treated by
those others. Although the principle works a-
symmetrically also, since people and circumstances are different as well as similar, the
remarkable regularities with which it can be
observed to operate symmetrically provide bases
for useful generalizations. Long experience
in teaching ethics to college students has led
me to formulate the following ten principles,
each available for research and rigorous testing, as principles that each wisely self-interested person can exploit for his own benefit.

Limiting statements to a particular kind of
interest each person typically has, namely,
interest in esteem or how he is rated in the
eyes of others, the ten principles may be exemplified as follows:

a. Esteem is essentially social. To be esteemed on must be esteemed by others.

b. To be esteemed by others, one must somehow do or be what others admire.

c. One naturally enjoys being admired. So,
when admired, one normally desires more such
admiration. He may do more of what others ad-
more and thereby receive more admiration.

d. Or he may desire continuation or increase
of such admiration without doing more. Desire
for more approval often shades imperceptibly
into desire for more approval than one will
receive.

e. Desire for more approval than one will
receive begets unfortunate consequences. A
person's belief that he deserves more esteem
than he receives implies distrust of the opin-
ions of others. Others, finding themselves

distrusted, hence disapproved and disesteemed, tend to reciprocate by disapproving such distrust. Excessive desire for self-esteem is self-defeating.

f. The principle of reciprocity apparently inherent in human nature operates both negatively and positively. Condemn me, and I will want to condemn you, at least for condemning me. Admire me, and I will admire you, at least for admiring me.

g. One may help to satisfy his desires for esteem (1) by not despising others and (2) by appreciating others. One may deliberately withhold disesteem and deliberately initiate esteem of others. Self-interestedness, or desiring what is best for one's self, should not be mistaken for selfishness, which consists in intending to obtain more than one deserves at the expense of others. The more you want to increase your esteem, the more unselfish, and the more generous, you should be in esteeming others.

h. The principle of reciprocity usually reflects sincerity and insincerity. If one evaluates others insincerely, his insincerity tends to be reciprocated.

i. The principle does not work with mathematical precision. Delay should be expected in receiving some rewards. When coming later, they often appear as surprises. If your gift was genuine, you expected no return; when returns arrive unexpectedly, they may appear as undeserved or as more than deserved. Of course, others may forget our appreciation of them even as we forget their appreciation of us. But people who practice the principle testify that they come out ahead in the long run.

j. To the extent that the principle does work, each person has within his own power a means for increasing the satisfaction of his interest in esteem.

How these ten principles operate relative to
other interests involving interpersonal interaction may be observed and, I believe, are wor-
thy of rigorous testing because, to the extent
of their reliabilities (i.e., probabilities),
they can be most important resources exploitable
for both wise personal self-development and wise
social developments. How and why the principle
works differently in different kinds of interpersonal and intersocial interactions needs demonstrating, for failure to observe also the
"other things which are not equal" when formulating and using the principle is conductive to
failure and to harmful results.[16]

3. Wise social development. Although each
person is essentially social, the numbers and
kinds of groups in which he participates, and
the roles he plays in each group, usually are
matters over which he has some control. Feelings of identification with some groups and opposition to other groups are foundational to
group participation. When a person has a choice
of whether to participate in another group, wise
self-interest calls for his weighing the apparent advantages and disadvantages of joining.
Among the many kinds of factors involved in
wise social development, I mention only two.

a. Numbers and kinds of groups. Problems
recur concerning joining too many groups, more
important groups, long-range vs. short-range
groups, complex vs. simple groups, regular and
rigoristic vs. flexible groups, etc., and especially concerning conflicting interests within and
between groups. Since conflicting interests of
groups of which one is a member become conflicting interests within one's self oftentimes, the
nature, significance and costs of such conflicts
are important factors to consider when joining
another group.

Problems concerning distributive justice occur in each group, so the more groups one joins

the more he involves himself in problems and
difficulties concerning distributive justice.
Problems concerning rights and duties of each
member, of each group relative to its members,
and of groups relative to each other, recur in
each group. Problems of minimal or required
conformity to each group's institutions recur.
Problems of whether a person is overextending
his capacity to perform his duties in each
group should be faced. So increased enlightenment regarding the nature, the costs, and the
responsibilities involved in joining groups as
well as anticipated benefits seems called for
in each person's wise social development. Yet,
given the plethora of varieties of groups, joining groups is often one of the easiest ways for
a person to expand his personality and the richness of the cultural complexes with which he
shapes it.

b. Roles in groups. One can participate in
a group only by having one or more roles to
play. Wisdom dictates relative passivity in
some groups, e.g., when one is a member of a
large television audience. But most wise self-
interested persons will become active agents in
one or more groups as a normal and healthy means
of personal development. Furthermore, I believe
that each person should want to accept some responsibility both for himself and for some others, as a normal part of a healthy life. Responsibility, understanding of which is another
important task of ethics as a science, has been
neglected in this work, partly because complexities involved in understanding its nature and
kinds prevent clarification in a summary treat-
tment and partly because I need more study of
it before proposing some hypotheses about it.[17]

But about one hypothesis I am very clear.
Persons who accept responsibilities that they
are able to bear can be observed to behave differently, to act more influentially, to act as

more substantial agents, to act with more confidence, and to enjoy their activities more
than before accepting them. One who accepts
responsibility normally thereby acquires authority, i.e., whatever authority is required for
carrying out the responsibility. Selves may
become more authoritative by accepting more responsibilities. More responsibilities are accepted normally when one obtains a position in
an occupational group, becomes an officer in a
group, or becomes a parent. Persons achieve
importance, and social recognition of importance,
by acquiring responsibilities, and, generally
speaking, the more important the responsibilities
the more importance normally attributed to persons bearing such responsibities. Thus social
development of a wisely self-interested person
can increase his importance, both in his own
eyes and in the eyes of others, by his acceptance of, and by excellence in bearing, responsibilities for the welfare of himself, of others
and of the group or groups in which he participates responsibly.

One may, of course, acquire responsibilities
that he is not able to bear or can bear only
deficiently or with great trouble. Wisdom calls
for not acquiring and for relinquishing responsibilities that one is not able to bear. Children
should be encouraged to achieve both more capacities and responsibilities as they mature; but
only those they can bear competently. The aged
should be encouraged to retire as their energies
decline; but only from those responsibilities
that they can no longer bear competently. The
importance of self-esteem and continuing enjoyment of life resulting from bearing responsibilities competently should not be underestimated
when seeking to be wisely self-interested.

4. Wise world development. Each person's
happiness often depends also on his abilities
to identify himself with many other things in

the rest of the world. Opportunities are endless. I do not believe that ethics as a science need begin by assuming any particular
kinds of identification as essential to happiness, but I do believe that it is a task of
ethics as a science to investigate, or to call
on other sciences that do investigate, both
whether any are essential to happiness and what
the probabilities are that increased happiness
will result from each of the many additional
kinds of identification.

Among the many different kinds of things
with which people sometimes feel identified
are animals, ranging from totems to pets. Some
persons feel identified with plants and "all
sentient beings," and some of these persons
subscribe to reincarnation of persons as animals, plants and gods. Some person feel identified with their cells, molecues, atoms and
subatomic particles. Some feel identified with
the earth ("earthdwellers"), some with our solar system, some with our galaxy, and some
with the whole universe. People report increased enjoyment from each of these kinds of
feelings of identification. There are so many
that most persons will want to be selective.
Yet persons who identify themselves too narrow-
ly tend to neglect some of the most enjoyable
values of life.

Problems of justice, retributive (recipro-
cative) and distributive, recur relative to
things in the rest of the world. Current concerns about ecology have emphasized these problems. Each person may ask himself: "Am I fair
in my treatment of the animals and plants with
which I come in contact?" "Does the world owe
me a living?" I refer now not to society, but
to Nature, or the rest of the world. "Is the
world treating me better or worse than I am
treating it, or them?" "How ought I conceive
myself and my best interests when considering

how much more in the universe I choose to feel
at one with?" People who are able to feel at
home in this world enjoy it more. Those who
feel alienated seem to enjoy it less, and the
more of the world from which they feel alienated the less they seem to enjoy it. Such people often dream of another, better world beyond.

   5. Wise whole life development. Although
some persons seem to be always fully occupied
with the problems that confront them day by day,
if one can take time to envision his whole life
in such away that he can foresee benefits possible from choosing one course of development
rather than another, he is likely to be willing
to make a responsible choice provided he has
sufficient understanding and information. Life
planning has its difficulties and benefits.
Among the difficulties are many uncertainties
about the future. Plans made **too early** in **life**,
i.e., from a childhood perspective, may lead
to living a whole lifetime fulfilling a child-
ish perspective. Plans made too late in life
lose the benefits of fuller and sounder prepara-
tions and the possibilities of longer and fuller
developments. Plans adopted too rigidly yield
disappointments when life situations require
flexibility. Plans adopted from a reductionistic perspective beget deficiency and whatever
troubles are encountered when interacting with
persons whose perspectives have been eliminated
or depreciated by the reduction involved.

   Wise planning of one's whole life faces reductionistic tendencies in another way. Some
locate their primary interests in self-development, some in interpersonal development, some
in social development, and some in rest-of-the-
world development. If genuine values exist at
all levels, does a person not shortchange himself by restricting his interests primarily to
any one of these kinds of development? Is not
some kind of balanced distribution of interests

at each of these four levels desirable in living one's life as a whole?

Inquiry into the ultimate values of life as
a whole belongs to religiology. Religion is
concern for one's ultimate values, the values
of his life as a whole. Religion is not, as
many hold, belief in God or gods. Such a mistaken conception results from hasty general-
ization from acquaintance with too few religions. When one becomes aware of the existence
of atheistic religions, such as Jainism and
Theravada Buddhism, and seemingly theistic
conceptions so divergent from Western theisms,
he becomes aware of a fundamental mistake. My
studies of the world;s religions[18] yield the
hypothesis, verified for me, that religion is
a person's concern for his ultimate values,
for the values of his life as a whole. If the
values of a person's life as a whole are his
most important values, and if he has obligations, conditional and actual, regarding real-
izing those values, then for him his religious
ethics are his most important ethics. Surely
wise self-interest does not stop short of concern for what is best for one's self in the
long run and on the whole.

Chapter IV

SOCIAL ETHICS

Social ethics is both like and different from
personal ethics.

On the one hand, groups and culture do not
exist apart from persons. Thus the whole purpose of groups is to serve the needs of persons.
Groups derive both their existence, natures and
values from persons. Intrinsic values exist in
persons, and they exist in groups only because
they exist in persons as members of groups. Culture, including all institutions, exists in persons and nowhere else. The purposes of culture
no matter how much expressed in terms of civili-
zations, empires, religions, races, class strug-
gle or human destiny, have their ultimate locus
in minds, values and interests of particular
persons.

On the other hand, each group existing long
enough to develop stability and to serve the
needs of persons reliably thereby automatically
develops a nature and stabilities of its own,
not apart from persons but in addition to
the natures and stabilities of the persons who
are its members. When this occurs, groups able
to become self-conscious through attention by
members and/or officers, tend to become aware
of their own natures and interests, of how to
develop awareness of self-interest, and of how
to realize it and improve it. To the extent
that groups also differ from persons, problems
in social ethics become different from those in
personal ethics. To the extent that culture,
including institutions, transcends persona and
controls persons, problems in social ethics
become different from those in personal ethics.

Thus ethics as a science has a twofold task
constantly, namely, concern about personal ethics and concern about social ethics. This task is

142

complicated by both constant interdependence
and interaction of groups and their culture
and the constant, but dynamic and variable,
interdependence of persons with their groups
and cultures. Here we focus attention first
on the nature of groups and then on the nature
of culture.

GROUPS

   1. The nature of groups. a. Essential conditions. Groups consist of persons conscious-
ly associating with each other, directly or indirectly. As a minimum, a group requires two
persons, although one may be asleep temporari-
ly. As a maximum, a group may include the whole
of mankind provided that persons are aware of
some minimum communication and that some of the
persons have feelings of identification with
all of the rest.   Concern here is limited to
human groups, although animals sometimes participate in human groups and associate in social
groups of their own.
   Conditions essential to the existence of human beings and to their conscious association
are conditions essential to the existene of
groups. One condition, awareness, seems a very
fragile basis for the existence of groups. But,
despite its seeming fragility, it is nevertheless sufficiently substantial to enable families,
communities, states, nations, races, religions,
industrial corporations and mighty armies to
exist, sometimes for centuries. It is the same
awareness on which science depends for its existence, for without awareness there would be
no science. But, both as fragile and as substantial, awareness is a basic condition of
social ethics.
   b. Kinds of variations. Groups have a temporal nature. Some have only an instantaneous
duration, as when two automobile drivers pass

each other on a highway speeding in opposite
directions. Some endure much longer than the
lifetimes of all of their members, as when a
nation celebrates its two hundredth anniversary.
I will not try to settle questions about how people who identify themselves with their ancestors
manage to communicate, although writers of many
ancient scriptures continue to communicate
their ideas to readers today. I have no ob-
jection to restricting social groups to persons
who are both living and communicating. Such
groups are at least actual. But questions
about how infrequently members can communicate
and still constitute a group, e.g., pen pals
writing once every five years, may result in
further definitional refinements. All of the
citizens of the United State are commonly regarded as constituting one group even though each
has seen and talked with only a few, perhaps a
few hundred or a few thousand, of them, but no
one has communicated directly with all of them.

Groups have members. Groups vary regarding
how much or how little each member's interests
are identified with them. The interests of members satisfied by casual groups often are minimal.
Many groups serve a single interest, such as a
gasoline station attendant and his client seeking fuel. Some groups serve all of the interests
of at least some of their members, as in an in-
fant-mother or infant-family group. Thus the
relative importance of groups to members varies
with how completely a person identifies his personal self-interests with those of his groups,
and this is likely to depend on how many functions
a group performs for him and how dependent he is
upon the group for the performance of such functions.

Groups change, by adding members and losing
members, by adding functions and terminating
functions, and by increasing or decreasing the
amounts and qualities of functions performed.

Most groups originate and terminate, although
some groups seem to have origins lost in history and some intend to continue forever. Some
groups help in the generation of other groups,
and some groups help in the termination of other groups.

The foregoing sketch of some of the conditions and variations constituting the nature of
groups is intended to depict some of the multiplicities of variables that must be taken into
consideration by a science of ethics. Despite
the improbability that we can find many similar
situations in which all "other things are equal,"
nevertheless it is possible to observe many kinds
of uniformities useful as principles for basic
statements of conditional oughts. For whenever
there are variables, there must be something
that is varying, something that can serve as a
basis for generalizations, including generalizations about variations. In describing the nature of groups as agents generating and encoun-
tering social oughts, it is better to be realistic about evident complexities and fragilities
than to indulge in simplifying reductionisms
that later reveal their inadequacies and cause
loss of confidence in the reliability of ethics
as a science.

2. Kinds of groups. One way to classify
groups is by the kinds of functions that they
perform as services to their members.

a. Two main kinds. Groups may be classified
roughly into those having more general purposes
and those having more specialized purposes.

(1) Those having more generalized purposes
are by nature multifunctional, and sometimes
omnifunctional in the sense that they have an
interest in, and would if they could accept
responsibility for serving all, or most, of the
needs of their members. These include mother-
child groups, intimate family groups, community
groups, and some states and nations. Such

groups tend to have geographical location and
extension, and often participate in hierarchical relations such that a nation has an interest
in satisfying the interests of its states which
have interests in satisfying the interests of
their communities which have interests in satisfying the interests of families which have
interests of persons who are their members.
Sometimes the interests of such hierarchies
duplicate each other or are shared by each
other and sometimes there is a division of labor such that some of the needs are served by
the national group (e.g., military protection)
and some by the local community (e.g., sewage
disposal).

(2) Groups having more specialized purposes
have more limited aims and have their natures
and purposes, and ethical problems, determined
largely by the special natures of their services.
Not only do we have groups that are primarily
economic, political, educational, religious and
recreational, but among economic groups we have
some that are devoted primarily to production,
exchange, transportation, storage, marketing,
consumption accounting, banking, insurance, re-
pairing, etc.

Difficulties with this rough classification
include tendencies of some general purpose groups
to specialize in various ways. Any division of
labor at different levels (nation, state, community, family) already constitutes specialization. Higher-level groups establish subgrous
(departments, bureaus, branches) to accomplish
some specialized purposes. Lower-level groups
sometimes associate for specialized purposes.
Many special interest groups (banks, insurance
companies, retail stores) are licenced by general purpose groups. Some special-interest
groups adopt multipurpose group interests in
order to accomplish their specialized purposes
(e.g., mining companies sometimes establish

company villages that provide most needed
services, and some churches establish monas-
teries and nunneries where all of the needs
of members are cared for).

Despite these difficulties of classification, we can observe that some of the kinds of
ethical problems typical of omnipurpose and of
special purpose groups differ. The omnipurpose
group has responsibility for keeping the total
welfare of persons in mind, and to carry out
such responsibility to the extent that it is
able. Actually the abilities of such groups
differ greatly. When abilities are lacking,
some of the functions serving needs of persons
cannot be performed. When this is the situation, primary ethical problems include how to
increase abilities, which services to perform,
and how well should services be performed.
The special-purpose group has responsibility
for performing its special function or functions. It tends to conceive its responsibilities primarily in terms of performing such
function or functions. Abilities differ here
also. But the ethical problems pertaining to
special function performance are comparatively
limited. At the same time, to the extent that
performance of a special function is essential
to personal and social welfare, ethical problems pertaining to the interrelations of special-purpose groups and omnipurpose groups also
exist as important kinds of problems that properly concern ethics as a science.

b. General purpose groups. Each of the many
general purpose groups has its own kinds of
ethical problems. Development of specialized
ethical sciences relative to each kind may be
expected. Primary group (including family)
ethics, community ethics, rural ethics, urban
ethics, megalopolitan ethics, national ethics
and world ethics all, despite their generalized
natures and purposes, have some special kinds

of problems calling for specialized attention,
research, conclusions and practices. Close
cooperation between ethics as a science and
each of the social sciences is itself an ethical obligation that becomes more obvious as our
understanding of the natures and kinds of groups
and of their difficulties and problems increases.

(1) Primary groups. The great importance for
ethics of the roles of primary groups, those
small, intimate, face-to-face groups in which
selves behave as whole persons, has already
been mentioned in Chapter III, pp. 99-104. Primary groups are efficient humanizers of animal
drives, major sources of self-conceptions,
originators of respect for others as intrinsic
values, nurseries of confidence in the natural-
ness of justice and the desirableness of fair
play, providers of intimate experience with
operations of the principle of reciprocity, and
establishers of habits of honesty, integrity,
tolerance and loyalty. Other groups, although
the may reenforce the ideals originating in
primary groups, depend on primary groups for
their humanizing, socializing and moralizing
services, and have a vested interest in the
perpetuation of such primary group services.

Primary groups are perhaps the most important to person as persons since there they not
only feel free to act as whole persons but are
able to do so because it is part of the nature
of primary groups to be interested in their welfare as whole persons. Primary groups are not
always able to provide for all of a person's
needs, but they do naturally have interests in
assuring that all such needs are provided for
as much as possible.

The importance of primary group services in
establishing in persons habits of acting rightly
becomes clearer as those habits are challenged,
modified, diluted and sometimes abandoned under
pressures of experiences in other groups. Many

148

people do retain their habits of integrity,
honesty, truthfulness, justice, loyalty and
generosity in all of the groups in which they
participate. But many more, or so it seems
today with the growth of megalopolitan and
global society, gradually discover that many
conflicts of interests are pursued selfishly
and that not all persons can be trusted to
exhibit primary group habits in non-primary
situations. Absence of such habits encourages,
sometimes creates, antagonisms which prevent
group cooperation or prevent fairness in the
distribution of a group's services. Some persons who, having trusted some others completely, have been seriously cheated, lose their
faith completely, distrust everyone, even when
they cannot become unjust themselves. Groups
lacking in willing moral cooperation are forced
to enact laws of minimum behavior requirements
and then to enforce them appropriately in order
to survive and function.

Decline in average percentages of time that
persons spend in primary groups may be part of
the cause of current trends embodying evidences
of growing demoralization. The little time
that city dwellers spend in their apartments
suggests that family living has itself become
something highly specialized, and too many living examples are discouraging others from enter-
ing marriage at all. Formerly, churches and
Sunday Schools emphasizing ethical ideals, supported primary group achievements; but loss of
confidence in sectarian doctrines has diminished this aid when it is not abandoned altogether.
Schools in primary group neighborhoods were
both fortunate in enjoying the moralizing services of the neighborhood and in contributing
very little to antagonisms that could not be
handled in ways that provided moral improvement in at least some pupils. But now some
monstrous urban schools, especially those in

districts populated by people impoverished by
unemployment, have become efficient training
groups for criminals and effective demoralizers.
Our larger general purpose groups, especially
states and the nation, have no significant plans
for long-range restoration of the moralizing
services of primary groups that are essential
to group living and which appear to be diminishing progressively. National, or state, or even
community, recognition of the establishment of
ethics as a science concerned with demonstrating
the oughtness of such restoration could help.

(2) Communities. Ethical problems, theoretical and practical, of communities are so various that generalizations ventured here must be
regarded as merely suggestions. Communities
range from those almost completely self-sustaining in function performance (as in tribal villages and some rural communities) to those quite
artificial sections of cities or their suburbs
that incorporate with very limited purposes.
Problems of deciding which functions (e.g.,
public safety, streets, water supply, sewage,
electricity, gas, telephone, education, libraries)
should be performed by the community are ethical
problems. Issues of whether it is better to supply community services by public or private
agencies are ethical issues. Ethics as a science
has no precommitment to any generalized preference for the performance of community functions
by public or private agencies. Experience thus
far seems to indicate that sometimes public performance is best and sometimes private performance is best. Ethics as a science is committed
to understanding, with the help of political,
economic and other social sciences, which is
best for each particular kind of situation and
when it is better to change from one to the other.

(3) Cities. Ethical problems of living in
cities have become so numerous and so complicated
that a special science, urbanology, has been

150

needed. No attempt will be made here to summarize these problems. But failure to make ethics as a science available as urban, metropolitan and magalopolitan groups multiply constitutes both a scientific and a moral deficiency on the part of both the scientific community and political leaders.

(4) States and nations. Questions about which functions ought to be performed by larger general purpose groups are essentially ethical questions. Many states and nations originated at particular times as a result of the common needs as understood at those times. To the extent that common needs remain the same, perpetuation of such states and nations seems best. As times and conditions change, questions about revision, readjustment and reallocation of function performance to meet new needs arise. Values of stability in complex organizations have great importance. But sometimes new values outweigh old ones and call for change. Experience seems to indicate that evolutionary rather than revolutionary change is less costly, although also sometimes conditions prevent needed evolution in ways that force changes to be more revolutionary. Political systems that encourage evolutionary change through legislative processes seem better, generally speaking, than those forcing use of more violent methods.

Problems regarding social justice, which exist at family and community levels, seem often to become progressively aggravated at city, state, national and world levels. To the extent that organizational functions at different levels can be isolated from each other, efforts to deal with them at each level may seem best. But as global life becomes increasingly interdependent regarding more and more needs, actual ethical problems increasingly involve inter-level intergovernmental under-

151

standing, decision and action. Vested interests of those favored by present systems inhibit or prevent adoption of wiser solutions to
common problems. Questions about continued
justification of favored vested interests,
when they become harmful obstacles to group
welfare, are among the most difficult practical
problems concerning which ethics as a science,
cooperating with political, economic and other
social sciences, should be called upon to provide understanding.

(5) World society. Shrinking globe, population explosion, wasteful exhaustion of limited resources, progressive pollution, threats
of nuclear holocaust, and increasingly intricate interdependence in the performance of
functions, all make world society a fact. Absence of some effective minimal world government continues to be a most serious deficiency
so far as wise collective solutions to the
above problems, now having reached crisis proportions, are concerned. The obviously devastating costliness to all of a Third World War
is such that most agree that we ought not to
permit it to occur. Yet perpetuation of the
arms race contributes to probabilities that it
will occur. Prevention of a Third World War,
or any war, for that matter, is a major ethical
problem facing mankind, and each nation, and
all other groups and persons having influence
on the course of future events.

Since the decisions of those who can increase
or decrease armaments endangering mankind are
ethical decisions, the ethical understandings
and convictions of those who make such decisions
are crucial factors regarding human survival
and welfare. Absence of sound ethical enlightenment regarding all human values and consequent
obligations (conditional oughts) promotes decisions based on narrower or short-range interests. Development and promotion of ethics as

a social science that can be called on to demonstrate, with the cooperation of all other social sciences, what is really best could help to prevent rash and devastating wars. Commitment to the use of scientific methods, which political leaders in all countries have been forced to recognize as best regarding technology for dealing with many kinds of problems, can be persuasive in promoting international cooperation when other methods, including bribery and prejudicial subsidies and threats of war, cannot. Of course, if scientific and political leaders in the United States do not recognize and support development of ethics as a science, it is not available for their use in influencing leaders of other nations.

The oughtness of public and private support for the development of ethics as a science becomes more evident as one becomes better acquainted with the nature of ethics as a science and with the numbers, magnitudes and urgency of practical ethical problems facing our nation and mankind.

c. Special purpose groups. Special purpose groups tend to become organized whenever a common interest can be serviced better, sometimes only, through persons cooperating in a group. Such groups, like all groups, normally come into being because they are good, i.e., are useful as means to human ends. Special purpose groups tend to perform needed services more efficiently, though they too are subject to cultural lag. Both the initiation and the perpetuation of special purpose groups involve ethical decisions. Such groups, once established, often add functions, compete with persons and other groups, special and general, for performing functions.

Questions arise about which groups should perform what functions. The ethical problems of simpler groups deciding about simpler

functions can be oberved to be comparatively
much less difficult than those of larger groups,
especially of higher-level groups, when they
must encounter the strongly established vested
interests of already existing general purpose
and special purpose groups.

The more complex society becomes, the more
complex each of the kinds of groups, including
political, economic and education, becomes, especially those performing functions essential
to personal and group welfare. Vitality, efficiency and ethical enlightenment in political
group decisions affect the vitality, efficiency
and ethical intelligence of decisions by economic, educational, medical and religious groups.

Today we seem to be witnessing progressive
degeneration, economic, educational, medical,
religious, political and ethical, with degeneration of each kind hastening degeneration in
all other kinds. Thus the urgency of recognizing the importance of both ethics as a general
science and of political ethics, economic ethics, educational ethics, medical ethics, religious ethics, etc., as specialized sciences increasingly interdependent with each other. Although each expert specialist is also an ethical
specialist in his own field, failure to recognize the increasing need for understanding the
ethics of interdependence in an age of increasing interdependencies is not only a general
deficiency but also diminishes the competence
of each specialist to the extent that his services are needed for the vital, efficient and
ethically intelligent services of other groups.

3. Group self-interest. I observe that
groups, like persons, are naturally self-interested and I propose a theory of enlightened and
wise self-interest as the most enlightened and
wise policy to adopt as a basis for ethics as
a science.

a. Nature of group self-interest. Each exist-

ing group naturally has interests in achieving
its purposes, fulfilling its functions and performing its services beneficially. Each group
has a natural interest in acting rightly, i.e.,
of intending to produce the best results for
itself in the long run. Again, what results
are best depend on the nature of the group and
its natural interests. How each group conceives
itself, i.e., how it is conceived by its members
or at least its responsible officers, determines
how it conceives its own best interests. Difficulties often occur when different members, or
different officers, disagree about such conception, interests and what is best. Furthermore,
the nature and interests of some groups change,
both from external and from internal causes.
Not all members or officers agree regarding
the changes.

Among normal kinds of group interests, except for those groups that terminate spontaneously or after a predetermined period because
they have temporary purposes, are interests in
survival, in stability, in perfection of its
services, in the morale of its members and officers. Among changes normal to group development, especially as division of functions
among officers becomes established and officers
devote more time to such functions, are improved services to officers. When officers
develop vested interests in their positions,
they often succeed in favoring themselves,
sometimes necessarily so, in ways that are at
the expense of other best services to members.
The larger the group and the more functions
it performs, the more naturally does it tend
to develop a bureaucracy with its typical
evils as well as benefits. Groups have interests in minimizing evils as well as in maximizing benefits.

   b. Kinds of interests. Interests of groups
may also be essential to their natures and

and functions and be non-essential, they may
be important and trivial, long-range and short-
range, more devoted to anticipatory satisfactions and less, recurring and unrepeatble, habitual and flexible, complex and simple, harmonizing and disharmonizing, and concerned with
optimzing values. (See Chapter III, pp. 120-123.)
Ethical issues regarding additional complications
of these kinds of interests for wisely self-interested groups will not detain us here. Emphasis here is limited to kinds of interests that
tend to be common to groups. In addition to
the interests determined by the kind of group,
whether general purpose or special purpose and
what are its particular purposes, we can observe
some kinds of interests typical of many kinds of
groups.

(1) Common to most groups of persons. Referring to groups composed of persons and not to
groups composed of other groups, we can observe
that each group normally has interests in:

(a) Its members as persons. Even in groups
most highly specialized, so that attention and
effort are focused on function performance, such
as electricity supply where officers and users
seldom meet, interest in the welfare of persons,
i.e., as whole persons, as well as members served,
is foundationally implicit at least. The larger
more specialized purpose groups become, the less
obvious, or at least the less attention paid to,
the interests of members as persons, unless decision makers have become especially enlightened. In primary groups, the interests of persons
continue to be primary.

(b) In its members as members. Membership in
a group normally involves some minimums and maxi-
mums of rights and duties, especially in more
formally organized groups. Normally self-interested groups have natural interests in serving
the interests of their members beneficially,
fairly, efficiently and maximally. Service to

members is the primary purpose, if not the
sole purpose, originating most groups.[1]

(c) In the group as a group. Group stability, survival and consequent organization for
service and survival are natural interests of
groups. Unless conditions conducive to group
service and survival occur naturally, as in
rural families, some kind of organization of
members and officers tends to be required.
The kind of organization which a group achieves
influences its abilities for survival and service. Thus each group has a natural self-interest in achieving a kind of organization conducive to its survival and service. Such organization normally includes some duties as well
as rights by members and officers.

(d) In the group's officers. Groups requiring officers, and especially larger groups
and multipurpose groups, necessarily develop
interests in the welfare of their officers.[2]
The more a group's survival and efficient service depends on efficient service by its officers, the more it has a vested interest in
their welfare, not only as officers but as persons. The more fully a person devotes himself
to serving as an officer, the more important
it is, both for the group and for himself, that
the group recognize that it has interests in
his welfare as a person. Persons who become
full-time officers of a group rightly acquire
rights to beneficial consideration as persons
as well as officers. A group has natural interests in the morale and willingness to serve,
as well as in the excellence of understanding
and skilled services, of its officers.

(e) Persons who are not members. Although
persons who are not members are not entitled
to a group's services, so long as persons who
are not members are potential members, are
actual beneficiaries of the group or are actually harmed by the group's actions, or are

potential beneficiaries or potential enemies
of the group, each self-interested group has
some interests relative to such persons.

(f) In other groups. Most groups composed
of persons have relations with other groups.
These relations may be of many kinds, as outlined in Section (2), below. Types of relations
include competition, cooperation, or both, both
as groups and in relations to their members.
When we observe that the ethics of each group's
self-interest in its members as persons, in its
members as members, in its group's nature, purpose and functions, and in its officers, are
compounded by the ethics of a group's interests
in other groups of many kinds, we can see that
ethics as a science has endless complexities
of kinds of self-interest to deal with. Wise
self-interested action by groups includes seeking enlightenment regarding all of these different kinds of interests normal to the nature of
most groups.

(2) Common to most groups as groups. Most
groups have relations with, and interests in,
(a) peer groups, (b) subgroups, and (c) higher-
level groups. Each such kind of interest tends
to generate its own kind of ethical problems.

(a) In relations with peer groups. Peer
groups are of two main kinds, those performing
the same kinds of functions for persons (either
for the same persons, e.g., competing grocery
stores, or for different persons, e.g., local
churches of different exclusive sects) and those
performing different kinds of functions for persons (either for the same persons, e.g., public
utilities such as those providing gas, electricity, water and sewage disposal, or for different persons, e.g., recreational groups, such
as those pertaining to golf, tennis, swimming,
hunting, skating, sailing, polo, opera, etc.,
serving persons with different preferences).
Problems of variable competition and coopera-

tion normally occur. Generalizations about conflicts of interests will be dealt with below, Section 4.

(b) In relations with subgroups. Many kinds of subgroups exist. Two main kinds are those that have organized themselves into a larger group (such as families incorporating a village or as baseball teams organizing a league) and those that have been organized by a larger group to serve one or more of its specialized purposes. Subgroups of the first kind tend to be more independent of than dependent on their larger groups and to determine the natures and rights and duties of their larger groups, at least originally. Groups of the second kind tend to be more dependent on than independent of their higher-level groups and to have their natures and rights and duties determined primarily by their higher-level groups, at least originally.

(c) In relations with higher-level groups. Higher-level groups are of two main kinds, as already indicated in the previous paragraph, namely, those organized from lower-level groups and those organizing subgroups for special purposes. Higher-level groups of the first kind have their natures and rights and duties determinied primarily by the subgroups from which they originated and on which they depend. Higher-level groups of the second kind usually are more independent of their subgroups which have their natures and rights and duties determined by their originating higher-level groups.

(d) In hierarchies of groups. Since some higher-level groups function also as subgroups of still-higher-level groups and since the numbers and complexities of hierarchical stacks of levels increase as people live more inter-dependently, the ethical,as well as economic and political, importance of group hierarchies

continues to increase. Since the natures of
some higher-level groups pertain primarily to
their services to other groups, including other higher-level or lower-level groups, and thus
less directly to persons, problems of officers
keeping in mind the ultimate reason for their
existing in services needed by persons, receive
variable treatment. Part of the importance of
ethics as a science is the need for providing
its enlightenment, with the aid of other social
sciences, regarding all of the actual duties
and rights of groups higher up in hierarchies
of groups. Problems of justice become increasingly complicated as hierarchies increase in
numbers of levels and numbers and kinds of
functions. Failure of officers responsible for
decisions, especially in the highest-level groups,
to choose and act with enlightened self-interest,
requiring consideration of the interests of all
persons as persons as well as all of the interdependent groups, can easily produce tremendous
harm for multiplicities of persons and groups.

4. Conflicts of interests. In addition to
conflicts of interests each person has merely
privately and conflicts of interests he has
relative to choosing whether or not to join
groups and which groups, his interests in the
nature and welfare of the groups of which he is
a member become, directly or indirectly, conflicts in his own interests. Focus here is on
the kinds of conflicts that normally occur in
groups as groups. The kinds of conflicts vary
with the kinds of groups, both kinds of general
purpose groups and kinds of special purpose
groups, and both internally, in relations with
its members and subgroups, and externally, in
relations with nonmembers, peer groups, and
higher-level groups.

a. Conflicts of groups with members. In addition to conflicts between a group's members
as persons (which may affect their relations

as members and their relations to the group)
and to conflicts between a group's members as
members (either relative to their services to
the group or the group's services to them,
which may cause problems regarding agreements
about the nature and rights and duties of the
group), conflicts centering in the nature of
groups include the following:

(1) Conflicts of a group's members as persons. Ethical questions about what is the
best division of a person's interests as a member versus all of his other interests are implicit in every membership of each person in
a group.

(2) Conflicts of groups with members. Ethical questions about the rights of members
and duties of groups to members are inherent
in group membership. Such questions may pertain to the rights of all members and the duties of a group to all members or the rights
of one or some members and the duties of a
group to one or some members.

(3) Conflicts of members with groups. Eth-
cial questions about the rights of groups and
the duties of members to groups are inherent
in group membership. Such questions may pertain to the rights of a group and the duties
of members relative to all members of the
group or to the rights of a group and the duties of one or some members of it.

(4) Conflicts of groups with officers. Eth-
Officers (including all employees) of groups
normally have more or less definite rights
and duties related to their performing functions
for their groups. Conflicts of interests of a
group with its officers occur whenever a group
wants more service from its officers than they
are prepared to give. Relations of groups with
officers are complicated by the fact that they
they have rights and duties as members of the
group and as persons as well as added rights

161

and duties as officers. Further complications
result from conflicts between officers, as officers, as members, and as persons. The evils
of exploitation of officers (including all employees) by groups are among the most difficult
problems that ethics as a science has to deal.

(5) Conflicts of officers with groups. When
officers feel mistreated by their group, they
tend to reciprocate in some way. Although re-
signation or dismissal removes or reduces such
conflicts in some groups, when officers become
professionally or occupationally employed by a
group, their long-range interests tend to create
more demands on their group than it originally
intended or is able to meet. Development of
bureaucracy, fringe benefits, tenure and union-
ization complicate, and sometimes institution-
alize, conflicts of officers with their groups.
When unions, justified by group mistreatment of
officers, become established powerfully, tendencies to pressure special interests of officers
beyond appropriate proportionate benefits from
a group, reverse injustice may occur. Problems
inherent in tendencies of unions to improve
benefits to officers (including all employees)
to become excessive with resulting evils are
among the most difficult with which ethics as
a science has to deal.

b. Conflicts internal to groups as groups.
Each group, once established, has its own nature and interests and naturally seeks what is
best for itself. Normally each encounters many
kinds of choices calling for decisions. Each
often encounters the following kinds of conflicts of interests, in addition to those mentioned above.

(1) Different kinds of interests conflict.
Groups normally have economic (financial),
political (system of control), educational (inform members) interests; and, for example,
sometimes educational interests cost more than

financial interests can support. When interests of different kinds conflict, groups as
groups must deal with them.

(2) Groups want more than they can have.
Tendencies in human nature to want what one
does not have tend also to generate wants for
more than one can have. These tendencies recur in groups as groups, whether from demands
by members, or officers or from unfortunate
circumstances in which groups find themselves.
When the evils of overdrawn accounts and deficit spending result in bankruptcy, disaster
follows. Englightened self-interest by groups
should prevent such disasters, but only by means
of enlightened understanding of sufficient
techniques for group self-control and of willingness to pursue a group's self-interest
wisely.

(3) Conflicts between subgroups. When
groups having interests of sufficient complexity that a division of labor among those performing its functions occurs and departments,
branches or bureaus develop, then competition
between the groups of persons organized to
perform such functions may occur as conflicts
of interests within the group. When special-
interest groups, cooperating as members of a
larger general-purpose group, pursue their own
interests in service by, or in control of, the
larger group, they often compete in ways constituting conflicts of interests of the larger
group. When one special-interest group obtains
an advantage compared with other special-interest groups, competition often endangers conflict. Increased enlightenment about both the
nature of groups and of normal consequences for
groups of subgroup conflicts should help to
reduce the evils of such conflicts.

c. Conflicts between groups. In addition
to the above, I mention conflicts between
peer groups and conflicts with higher-level

groups.

(1) Conflicts between peer groups. Two families, two department stores, two universities, two cities, two states, two nations, etc., may have conflicting interests. When both of two groups want what can be had by only one, group conflict exists. When one attains a benefit thereby depriving the other, evil exists for the other. To the extent that reciprocating tendencies also exist, further conflict may be expected. The ethics of peer group conflicts includes constant dangers that, when officers concentrate attention on the interests of the group as a group, the interests of its members as members and as persons tend to be neglected somewhat, and, often, are severely frustrated.

For example, two nations at war, or even threatening war, tend to increase their efforts and expenses for war conduct or preparation and, later, war debts in ways that withdraw resources from other services. How much food, housing, health, education, etc., could be purchased if the costs of wars and of preparedness (arms races) and debts were available for them? Earlier nations had some chance of winning. "To the victor belongs the spoils." Now Hiroshima-like holocaust prospects from national overkill capacities predict that "Nobody wins." Not spoils, but only the spoiled, will remain. Human extinction is clearly a possibility. The ethics of war, including enmity, arms races, battle conduct, treatment of prisoners and conquered people, distribution of costs, including debts, are extremely complex. Development of ethics as a science recognized by inimical nations could be a major means for preventing wars and even for eliminating war as a way for trying to settle conflicts between nations.

(2) Conflicts with higher-level groups. Conflicts between one group and a higher-level group differ greatly depending on whether the

higher-level group is more dependent on its
lower-level groups or whether they are more
dependent on it. Such conflicts become more
complicated when a group has interest in,
and conflicts with, several higher-level groups
in an ascending hierarchy. When, as in more
democratically constructed hierarchies, each
higher-level group comes into being primarily
to serve the needs of lower-level groups, it
depends on them for its sources of stability,
purpose, functions, and rights and duties.
When, as in more dictatorially constructed
hierarchies, each lower-level group is designed to serve the needs of higher-level
groups, it depends on them for its sources of
stability, purpose, functions, and rights and
duties. Although examples of both kinds of
hierarchies can be found, actually existing
hierarchies tend to be variable mixtures of
the two types, especially since some groups
at some levels have become established more
stably, prosperously, powerfully and function-
ally.

Ethical problems in understanding and dealing with inter-level conficts, especially
multi-level conflicts, include understanding
and evaluating the relative merits of a type
of hierarchy in which groups of each level
have primary functions on which all other levels depend. Understanding which functions can
be performed most beneficially, and most efficiently, by groups at which level is a major
task for political ethics. Then, efforts of
groups at one level, whether families, pre-
cincts, cities, counties, states, nations or
the world society, will be seen as excessive
whenever they appropriate functions more beneficially performed by groups of other levels
(i.e., other things being equal).

As human existence becomes in fact more
interdependent globally, problems of deciding

which functions are best performed by a world
government become more crucial, and many such
problems cannot be settled finally without
some experience and experiment which itself may
be very costly. Yet, especially considering
the wastes and costs and devastating prospects
of war, costs of such experiments probably will
be much less. Self-interest of mankind is a
genuine kind of group self-interest that today
seems not only neglected but endangered by prospects of total extinction because the policies
practiced by nationalistic and other powerful
special-interest groups lack the enlightenment
regarding all of their interests needed to
achieve a wiser self-interested, and a less-
selfish and narrower-self-interested, consequence.

The fates of personal interests, complexified
by membership, directly or indirectly, in conflicts between groups at several levels of our
hierarchies, are multifarious. But every costly conflict between groups tends to have some
cost effects in the lives of all members as persons. So each wisely self-interested person in
our intricately complicated multileveled society
has a stake in reducing unnecessary conflicts
between groups, inter-level group conflicts, as
well as peer-group conflicts. Development of
ethics as a science is something in which each
enlightened and wisely self-interested person
has a fundamental interest.

5. Rights and duties. Conflicts of interests commonly give rise to questions about rights
and duties of groups as well as of persons.
Understanding the natures and kinds of rights
and duties of persons and groups is a task central to ethics as a science. Although groups
as groups do have rights and duties, the primary locus of rights and duties is in persons.
Since I neglected to discuss rights and duties
of persons in the Chapter on Personal Ethics,
I must now make up for that neglect before

proceeding.

a. Nature of duties.

A duty is something owed. I have neglected to mention duties because I regard the words "duties," "obligations" and "oughts" as synonyms, even if we use the words "duties" and "obligations" more often in social contexts and "oughts" more often in personal contexts. Just as we have actual and conditional oughts, so we have actual and conditional duties and obligations.

(1) Personal duties. Just as oughtness consists in the power that an apparently greater good has over an apparently lesser good in compelling our choices, so a person's duty, on any occasion, is determined by what appears to him to be the better or best decision and course of action. The ultimate basis of a person's duty is the intrinsic values constituting his life and the possibilities for optimizing those values. Each person's duty is first of all to himself as an embodiment of intrinsic values, actually and potentially, and to their improvement and optimization.

Because each person is not only essentially social but also very largely social in his nature and interests, a very large share of his values, and thus of his duties to himself, are social in nature. To the extent that a person can increase his values through participation in groups, both through more groups and more participation, and through more kinds of groups and more kinds of participation, he has a duty to himself to do so if and when he can. To the extent that a person suffers sufficient decrease in values by participating in groups of whatever kind, he has a duty to himself to withdraw if he can. Some groups are more difficult to withdraw from (infants from families, blacks, etc., from races, prisoners from nations). Some groups are more difficult to join (exclusive class, caste, race and professional groups). But

where capacities and opportunities exist for
increasing one's values through group participation, each wisely self-interested person has
a duty to himself to pursue his interests
through such participation.

(2) Social duties. When a person becomes a
member of a group, doing his duty to himself
by joining a group promising additional values
for him, he usually acquires not only additional
specific duties to himself to make use of the
services performed by the group but also duties
to the group. A person's duties to groups tend
to be of three kinds.

(a) Duties to other members of a group. By
acquiring membership in a group, a person acquires duties to other members of the group,
both relative to their membership and to them
as persons. They too are persons having intrinsic and other values, including rights to benefit from the services performed by the group.

(b) Duties to the group as a group. When a
group depends for its existence, nature and efficient functioning upon support by its members,
each member has a duty to contribute his share
to such support.

(c) Sharing duties of the group as a group.
Each group has its one several kinds of duties
as a group (outlined in the next section). To
the extent that group membership involves sharing some or all duties of that group as a group,
a person becoming a member acquires a duty to
contribute his share of support to the group.

Each person should, of course, weigh all of
the kinds of values and disvalues of acquiring
several additional duties when voluntarily joining a group. He has a duty (conditional ought)
to evaluate such additional duties before joining a group. One function of ethics as a science (with aid from other social sciences) is
to make persons more fully aware and kinds and
numbers of duties normal to group membership.

168

(3) Duties of a group. Each group has its own nature, purpose, functions and duties as a group. These include:

(a) Duties to members. Each group has a duty to serve its members in ways appropriate to its nature and functions. Where member participation in group decisions is a member's right and duty, a group has a duty to make such participation possible. It also has duties to its members as persons, at least to the extent that it does not jeopardize or unfairly harm their interests as persons.

(b) Duties to itself as a group. Groups differ in nature, purpose, functions, services, duration, numbers of members, numbers and kinds of officers, and interrelations with other groups. But regardless of such variations, each group naturally has duties to itself as a group to survive and prosper in the sense that it performs its beneficial services efficiently. A wisely self-interested group's first duty is to itself. **It chooses and acts** rightly when and because it intends what is best for itself in the long run. Again, what is best for a group will depend on how the group is conceived. Difficulties occur when different members conceive the group's nature and purposes, and thus interests and values, differently. A primary duty (conditional ought) of persons responsible for introducing or reducing functions of a group is also to clarify, and to inform members and others, of such changes.

Since a group is constituted by its members, including any officers, its primary interests include services to its members. A wisely-self-interested group continues to recognize this primary interest. Whenever officers of a group responsible for pursuing a group's interests neglect the relevant interests of members in any way, they neglect the group's primary self-interest. Whenever officers, who must expect to have interests as persons and as members as well as officers, pursue their personal interests at the expense of the group's interests, they become inimical to the group's doing its duty to itself in achieving what is best for itself as a group.

(c) Duties to others. A group's duties to others may be of many kinds:

Duties to other persons. Persons who are not members of a group may be benefited or harmed by the group's decisions and actions. It has duties especially to those persons who may become desired members and to those who are or may become inimical to the group's interests.

Duties to peer groups. Duties differ somewhat relative to peer groups cooperatively supplementing a group's services and to peer groups competing for performing the same kinds of services. They differ relative to general purpose and to special purpose groups.

Duties to higher-level groups. Groups too become members of groups, and acquire duties, often of several kinds, by such memberships. When a group of groups becomes a member of a still higher-level group, additional duties normally develop for each group and, more ultimately, for its members.

Issues involved in duties of groups will be discussed more fully below when rights of groups are considered.

b. Nature of rights. A right is something owned. A right is a claim regarding a benefit, i.e., the enjoyment of some good or relief from suffering some evil. The ultimate bases of rights are the intrinsic values embodied in persons and their genuine potentialities for actualizing more intrinsic goods. Yet most, if not all, rights are also social, inherently social. Rights are social in the sense that

if one person has a right then others have
duties to respect that right. In this sense,
rights involve duties. "One person's right
is another person's duty." In this sense,
rights and duties are by nature correlative.

(1) How do rights originate? Human rights
originate, first of all, by being caused to
exist by all of the causes of human beings
and their personal and social development.
Second, useful insights into origins may result from distinguishing between natural and
social origins. This distinction cannot be
very sharp because persons are naturally social and any society itself originated naturally
as an extended development of human nature.

(a) Social origins. Some persons advocate
that all rights are social in origin and nature. Not only do groups have rights but many
rights acquired by persons result from group
decisions. Most legislation is intended to
state or newly define the rights and duties
of persons and/or groups. Fines or incarcer-
ation often are assessed on those failing to
do their group-defined duties to protect the
group-defined rights of others. At least some,
if not all, rights have social origins.

But what gives a group a right to determine
other rights? What is the origin of a group's
right to decide social rights and duties? Groups
are composed of persons, and the natures of
groups, including their nature as rights-decid-
ing agencies, are derived from the natures of
the persons composing them. Of course, persons
also have natures that are inherently socialized, so any amounts or proportions of the
origins of rights attributable to the natures
of persons in addition to their social natures
must remain somewhat speculative. Some observations seem appropriate.

(b) Natural origins. I support the hypothesis that human rights originate in human nature.

This may be called a "natural rights" hypothesis. I do not support reductionistic conceptions of human nature (e.g., as a Platonic Form, an Aristotelian fixed species, a Christian sinner, a Hindu purusha, a Freudian libido, an Existentialist existenz, or a Cybernetic feedback mechanism) but advocate that the truest and most useful conception of human nature is that discovered by scientific observations, inductive generalizations, and hypotheses based on evidences from, and conclusions from, all of the sciences. As scientists learn more about different parts of the nature of persons and groups, including any new kinds of persons and groups that may yet come into existence, our conception of human nature should become more refined and a more reliable basis for understanding the nature of human rights. Ethics as a science has to work with the knowledge of natures provided by the sciences of its time.

Human nature as a product of biological evolution, involving adaptations to varieties of environments and resources available for survival and development, is partly well known. Persons must breath, eat, excrete, have clothing and shelter, protection from animal and other enemies, as minimums. These constitute needs which are basic to survival and exist as bases for ideas about human rights. The fact that biological development has incorporated feelings of enjoyment and suffering into some organs of adaptive response provides one basis in human nature of making decisions. These feelings, originating historically in adaptive responses, function as experiences of intrinsic values, and serve as bases for ideas about human rights. The end-in-itself character of feelings embodied in persons associated with their natural interests in survival, adaptation, development and expansion is the ultimate basis for human rights. These bases, thus, have a natural origin in the sense that they originate in, or that they originated along with the origination of, human nature.

The role of environmental factors in survival, adaptation, development and expansion of human nature should not be overlooked, for many of them have made, and continue to make, essential contributions to how human nature develops and survives. Current concerns about ecology serve as evidence of their importance. So the kinds of human rights that will be considered minimal will depend in part on the kinds of environmental factors affecting human survival, adaptation, development and expansion. Thus the sources of natural rights, i.e., those having their origins in human nature, are to be found in environmental factors inherent in human biological development. Complexities of factors both in biological development and environmental conditions contributed to the development of groups and thus to the nature and kinds of groups and to the nature and kinds of rights that have their origins in groups. Groups too have natures, so I support a natural rights hypothesis about the origins of group rights and duties to help decide some rights and duties of persons. Understanding social evolution as well as biological evolution as contributing to the existence and nature of human rights, both natural and social (or social as an additional natural development), is itself to understanding needed by an adequate science of ethics.

(2) Relations to duties. Both rights and duties have both natural and social origins. But do duties originate in rights, do rights originate in duties, do they originate together, do they originate from different sources, or do they originate variously, i.e., sometimes rights from duties and sometimes duties from

rights?

I treated duties first, partly to make the
point that naturally self-interested persons
naturally develop interests in optimizing values and that such interests involve choices and
thus oughts, obligations or duties. Duties
originate as obvious self-interested obligations
to choose what appears to be best for one's self
in the long run. Each person's duty is first to
himself. Persons have some duties to themselves
merely as persons. ("I ought to move so as to
stop a pain.") Does a person's duty to himself
merely as a person, e.g., has a duty to move so
as to stop a pain, involve also a right to move
so as to stop the pain, or a right to do his
duty to himself? I refer now not to group-
granted rights but to a right inherent in his
duty. Does a person always have a right to do
his duty, even merely as a person?

Persons have some duties to themselves as
social, i.e., whenever each associates with another person. One has a duty to do what is
best for himself through his association with
another. Since the other person also has values in which he is interested, when one can
achieve what is best by sharing goods with another or by reciprocating goods with the other,
then he has a duty to himself to do so. But
does this duty to seek what is best for himself
give him a right to do so? Or does his right
to do so, in such association, derive from the
permission granted by the other who has his own
duty to himself to grant such a right because
this will result in what is best for him? Do
the rights that associating persons grant each
other result from their own duties to do what
is best for themselves through such association?
Do such rights originate in such duties.

When I recognize another's right which it is
my duty to respect, my duty seems to originate
in his right. But it also originates in my

174

belief that it is best for me in the long run
to respect that right. Thus my duty to respect
another's right has a double origin, both in
his right to do his duty to himself through
having his right respected and in my duty to
do what I believe is best for me in the long
run. Again duties seem prior to rights, and
rights seem to originate in such duties.

When two people associate, one person having a right normally involves the other person
having a duty to respect that right. The apparent origin of many of our duties to others
in the rights of others seems so obvious and
so common to many that they adopt the mistaken
view that duties are by nature always only
duties to others. When this is so, persons
tend to be uninterested in, or to take a negative interest in, duties. But when one is
aware that one's duty is always first to do
what is best for himself and that his duties
to others, including his duties to respect the
rights of others, are extensions of his duties
to himself, he is more likely to take a positive attitude toward his duties, including his
duties to respect the rights of others. But
such awareness requires much more understanding of human nature, including its social nature, and of the nature of groups, than many
people acquire.

If, in a waiting room, I pool money with
another to purchase a candy bar and I have
right to half of the candy bar that we have
jointly purchased, then my associate has a
duty to give me half. His duty originates,
at least partly, in my right to half. But he
eats the whole candy bar, depriving me of my
right. What happened to my right? It ceased,
actually, when the bar was eaten. I may claim
that I still have a right to half, but this
right is only a conditional right, and now a
conditional right for which the conditions

for actualizing do not exist. Although the rights of some are understood to entail duties to others, awareness of those duties does not automatically engender in others feelings of duty sufficient to guarantee their fulfillment. The power that any right has is to be found in its ability to originate duties, feelings of oughtness involving feelings of compulsion to choose and to act so as to respect them or fulfill them. Duties are compulsive, but not rights. Rights have no power of self-enforcement merely by themselves; they require production of feelings of duty. So rights not only originate in duties; they depend on duties for their actualization. In these ways, apparently, rights seem to depend on duties much more than duties depend on rights.

(3) Group rights. One consequence of living in groups, whether inherited or initiated, is that additional duties and rights normally inhere in them. Groups too have natures, determined by the natures of their members and by the kinds of purposes and functions they are called upon to perform. Just as each group normally involves duties of members to each other as members and as persons and to the group as a group, and duties of the group as a group to its members as members and as persons, to other peer groups, and to higher-level groups and subgroups if any, so each group normally involves rights relative to each of these kinds of duties. Each person normally has a right to do each of his duties and a right to have others, the group, and other groups do their duties to him. The group has a right to do all of its duties and a right to have all of the various duties done to it. Ethics as a science has a complicated task in understanding all of these kinds of rights and of discovering principles regarding their variable importance and relative   likelihood of

176
fulfillment.

One characteristic of the rights of organized groups, in addition to rights believed present in more casual association, is that some rights and duties are more definitely defined, more clearly contractual, and more powerfully enforced. Although groups vary greatly in the importance given to assurance that rights will be respected, long-enduring general purpose groups with established mores often impose penalties for immoralities and newly organized political groups and licensed special-purpose groups normally specify rights and duties of groups and members in contracts and charters with specific penalties for violations of contractual rights. Legislators, aided by administrators and judges, are busy creating new laws aimed at improving functions and services of groups as well as additional services to groups by members as needed. The quantities and costs of police, courts, prisons, etc., are evidence of efforts put forth by groups to enforce rights, i.e., that persons or corporations do their duties in respecting rights. But the rights enacted by groups have their origins in the need for laws designed to promote the welfare of the group which is a primary duty of the group. Although officers have duties to enforce rights, and those duties originate in the establishment of those rights, those rights were established by legislators presumably doing their duty to improve group welfare. Group rights also seem more dependent on group duties than group duties depend on group rights.

The enormous and continuous clamor in the media regarding persons and groups demanding their rights, and complaints about violations of their rights, is partly a product of, and in turn contributes to, a willingness of people to emphasize more concern for their rights than

for their duties. Such concern implies that
they are more interested in having other people
do their duties. Such concern implies more interest in benefiting from rights requiring duties by others than in exerting efforts to do
those duties reqired so that others may benefit
from their rights. Absence of, and indifference
to, social responsibility has gained sufficient
adherence in the United States so that even national Congressmen have joined antiestablish-
ment anarchists in proclaiming rights without
regard for the need for attending to correlative
duties. Recent efforts to pass the Equal Rights
Amendment to the U.S. Constitution has met with
unexpected opposition. If rights depend on duties more than duties depend on rights, then the
efforts may have succeded better if it had been
named the "Equal Duties Amendment." Stress on
rights without duties undermines the moral sound-
ness of any social system. A major task of ethics as a science is to aid educators, legislators, media reporters and others to understand
their own duties as contributers to needs for
understanding that self-interested groups, and
persons, ought willingly to emphasize duties
more than rights since, apparently, rights depend for their origins and fulfillments on duties much more than duties depend on rights.

(4) Conflicts of rights. Sometimes persons
and groups have rights that conflict withe each
other, so that fulfillment of one will prevent
fulfillment of another. What happens then? And
what implications do what happens have for understanding the nature of rights?

For example, I have a right to play basketball and to go to the movies tonight. But I
cannot do both. When I choose to actualize my
right to go to the movies, what happens to my
right to play basketball? Do I still have such
a right? Or do I not have a right to all of my
rights?

For example, a nation has a right to protect itself and to support armed forces and
has a right to educate its citizens. But its
income and budget permit fulfilling only one
of its two rights. What happens to the unful-
filled right? Does a nation have a duty to
fulfill all of its rights? It does not have
an actual duty to do what it cannot do.

(5) Conditional rights. Some rights are
actual and actualized. ("I have a right to
sit in the office chair in which I am now sit-
ting.") Some rights are conditional. ("You
may park if you can find a parking place.")
What happens to conditional rights when not
actualized? In the foregoing examples of
conflicts where rights are not actualized, the
rights did exist as conditional rights. But
absence of sufficient other conditions to bring
about actualization resulted in nonactualiza-
tion. Although having conditional rights,
which may be actualized if sufficient other
conditions cooperate, may be better than not
having conditional rights, other things being
equal, having conditional rights that never
become actualized are not worth much as rights.

Although persons and groups may easily develop too much concern about their rights, to
have multiplicities of conditional rights only
a few of which ever become actualized tends to
reduce interests in such rights. Some minimal
ratio between having conditional rights and
having them actualized may be discovered by
ethical research as essential to normally
healthy respect for having rights.

The quantities of kinds of conditional rights
are so great that ethics, cooperating with all
other social sciences, at least, must devote
much time and effort to helping make them clear
and to make clear also the benefits and harms
that come from them. Just as a person or a
group may have too many duties, so a person

or a group may have too many rights. When conditional rights entail duties to maintain them even though many of them are never actualized, the costs (evils) of having such rights may be greater than the benefits. When so, then a person or group has an obligation (conditional ought or duty, and also a conditional right) to reduce or eliminate such rights. Thus ethics as a science has a double task relative to conditional rights, i.e., to understand both when it is better to increase them and when it is better to decrease them. It is much easier for a group to decrease the conditional rights of its members than to increase their actual rights, since conditional rights may be decreased by legislation whereas most actual rights require something additional, usually money, often unobtainable even by deficit spending.

c. Correlativity of rights and duties. We observed earlier that one person's right involves duties in others to respect that right. The same is true for groups. A group having rights involves duties in others; its right to support by its members involves duties in its members to support it, and its rights relative to other groups involve duties in other groups to respect its rights.

The problems involved in understanding the nature and kinds and probabilities of actualization of rights and duties where rights and duties appear to be correlative are among the most difficult, and at the same time among the most important, confronting ethics as a science. I shall summarize some difficulties first and then try to evaluate their importance.

(1) Difficulties. Several kinds of difficulties exist.

(a) We have already observed that rights often seem to depend on duties more than duties depend on rights. Where is the correlativity?

(b) We have already observed that declared

rights often go unactualized, so that having
a conditional right carries no guarantees
that others will do their duties in actualizing
it. Rights exist as actual only when others
are actually doing their correlative duties.
Rights exist as conditional oughts when agreements about rights and correlative duties exist.
But when conditional rights are not actualized,
no actual correlativity between such conditional
rights and actual duties exist.

(c) When a person acquires a right that involves a duty of others to respect it, how many
others acquire that duty? One? (So that for
one right there is, correlatively, one duty?)
Many? (How many?) Everyone in the world?
(Do persons unfamiliar with that right still
acquire a duty to respect it?) Only those who
come in contact with him relative to that right?

If acquiring a right by one person involves
many others acquiring correlative duties, do
duties thus multiply faster than rights whenever a new right is acquired? Even when correlativity exists in the sense that one person's right involves a duty in many other persons to respect it, no correlativity exists in
the sense that one right (a right in one person) involves many duties (one duty in each
of many persons).

(d) When one person acquires a right involving duties of many others to respect it, are
the duties of all such others equal? Since
people differ in their abilities and each has
no actual duty to do what he is unable to do,
the duties which a right involves in many
others are often variable rather than equal.
Lack of equality in such abilities is another
kind of lack of correlativity. This lack is
exemplified also when a group acquires a right
relative to its members when its members vary
in their abilities to respect that right. It
is exemplified also when a group acquires a

right relative to many other groups that differ in their abilities to respect that right.

(e) Correlativity of rights and duties is
interinvolved with another problem or, rather,
three other problems: equalities of rights,
equalities of duties, and correlativities between these two equalities. That is, in addition to one's person's right involving another
person's duty, does one person's having a
right involve another person, or many other
persons, in also having an equal right involving other person's duties? Does one person's
duty to respect another person's right involve
that other person in an equal duty to respect
the first person's right? Do equal rights, in
this sense, and equal duties, in this sense,
involve each other correlatively? These problems are dealt with in the next section on
justice. But they are mentioned here as difficulties involved in understanding the nature of
correlativity of rights and duties. Additional
difficulties involved in the existence of unequal rights and of unequal duties function also
as factors contributing to making rights and
duties noncorrelative.

(2) Importance. Despite the difficulties,
recognition of, and acceptance of, some correlativity between rights and duties is essential
to group living. If having a right entails no
one in a duty to respect that right, that right
does not exist actually. If group living involves rights, then it involves correlative duties. So ethics, together with political science and the other social sciences, is saddled
with the task of understanding the problems involved in the correlativity and lack of it essential to group living. Absence of competent
understanding, explaining and recommending improvements regarding correlativity constitutes
a deficiency in ethics, in political science,
in the policy sciences and in national and in-

ternational political practice. Urgent support for research regarding such correlativity
is in our national interest.

The magnitude of the importance of such research will be seen more clearly if we recall
that the problems recur at each level of groups
in our social and political hierarchies as well
as between groups at different levels, that
problems regarding correlativities multiply
with increasing population, increasingly interdependent economic, political and other group
functions, with increasingly impersonal interrelations and agencies for decision, and with
the increasing dangers and costs of disruptions
in group living. Awareness of the importance
of the problem, stated generally in the foregoing, increases when we recall the many different kinds of rights, including many specific kinds of rights.

Rights are of many kinds: temporary and
permanent, unique and universal, personal and
social, simple and complex, innate and acquired,
natural and artificial, earned and unearned,
and apparent and real. Specific rights are
of many kinds: economic, political, educational, medical, etc., including all specialties.
Specialists are naturally involved in specialized rights and duties and correlativities.
Without some degree of reliability of policies
and practices of correlativity in each specialty, scientific, technical and occupational,
group activity would collapse.

6. Justice. No problems are more central
to social ethics and political science than
those involved in understanding the theory
and practice of justice. Justice is of two
main types: distributive and retributive.
Each has its own kinds of problems and principles as well as sharing some problems and
principles. Problems of both kinds occur
normally in every group, though they tend to

become more complicated as groups increase in
size, numbers of functions, durations of institutional structures, rigidity and quantity
of vested interests, scarcity of resources, and
enlightened understanding by more members.

Common to both kinds are problems related to
understanding the nature of equality. Justice
involves equality. Distributive justice involves distributing benefits or costs equally.
Retributive justice involves giving and getting
equally. Problems concerning the nature of justice and of acting justly would be comparatively simple if there were no differences. But
differences, many kinds of differences, exist
as parts of most situations in which concern
about justice exists.

That justice involves treating equals equally is obvious. But people are also unequal.
Does justice involve treating unequals equally
also? Much popular clamor about equal rights
has presumed that people who are equal in some
respects are equal also in some other respects,
and perhaps in all respects, and that people
who are unequal in some respects should nevertheless be treated as equal in those respects.
Much confused thinking about the nature of justice prevails. An important task of ethics as
a science is not only to achieve clear understanding about the nature of justice but also
to help make that understanding available both
to those responsible for policy decisions and
those responsible for popular education.

A clearer understanding of the nature of
justice involves treating equals equally and
unequals unequally, i.e., equally unequally.
A person has as much right to have his unique-
ly individual differences respected as his
samenesses with other people. An infant should
not be required to manage a corporation. A man
should not be required to give birth to children.
A pauper should not be required to pay taxes.

A botanist should not be required to perform
as a physicist. Persons differ in their
abilities and justice surely does not require
that persons do what they are not able to do.

Policies regarding justice may be stated as
conditional policies. That is, "in so far as
persons are alike in any respects, they should
be treated alike, other things being equal."
One may proclaim ideals about people being
more alike than they are; however in a culture
emphasizing individualism and individual differences, many persons seem both to idealize
that, and to act as if, people are more different than they are. The policy that, "in
so far as persons are different in any respects, they should be treated differently
(equally differently) in those respects, other
things being equal," seems equally obvious to
me. Or, "in so far as people are equal they
should be treated equally and in so far as
people are different they should be treated
differently (equally differently), other things
being equal," is a policy that I believe will
be found to be both most obviously clear and
a most enlightened policy by ethics as a science.

Once the obviousness of this policy is
recognized, then problems of justice become
more and more factual problems about the actual natures of persons and about ways in which
they are alike and different and how differences can be treated equally differently. For
factual information about the natures of persons again ethics as a science urges a study
of all other relevant sciences. But the problem of understanding how to treat unequals
equally unequally, even though this is every-
body's problem, is one with which ethics as
a science must continue to grapple. One difficulty in trying to treat differences as equally different is that, when two persons are dif-

ferent and unequal, no principle of sameness
or equality inheres in such differences and
inequalities. Probably the best that one can
do is to intend to be as fair as seems possible,
and then not to worry too much about the problem.

Another important problem, already inherent
in the foregoing, is that, desirable as justice
is, when efforts to achieve justice cost more
than the benefits attained, the value of such
justice must be weighed against the disvalues
of the efforts involved. As the costs of
achieving increasingly precise degrees of justice grow, a process of diminishing returns
often eventually results in costs that outweigh
the benefits. Although variations regarding
kinds of justice problems are to be expected,
if researchable generalizations about some best
cutoff point in quests for increasing precision
are developed and tested as reliable, then
ethics as a science will have provided a very
useful service.

This problem becomes magnified when ethicists
are confronted with problems of understanding
justice on larger scales, e.g., nationally, in-
ternationally, and at the world level. For if
the costs of seeking precision in justice increase as groups grow larger, more complex and
more interdependent, then studies of differenti-
als regarding cutoff points at different levels
(sizes, complexities, interdependencies) are
called for. Whereas in a children's group, justice may require careful division of pennies,
justice at municipal levels may be unable to
extend precision beyond hundreds of dollars,
at state levels beyond thousands of dollars,
at national levels beyond millions of dollars,
and at the world beyond billions of dollars.
To persons seeking justice at lower levels, the
seeming insensitivity, but possible incompetence,
of decisions at higher levels may appear quite
unjust. But if there are limits of manageabil-

ity in larger organiziations, and thus limits
regarding how much precision in justice for
higher-level groups is possible, then these
limits must be recognized as factors in the
nature and kinds of justice that are possible
for some kinds of groups. Distinctions between macroethics and microethics may develop,
and different policies regarding what kinds of
precision are possible at different levels may
be recognized. But the task of seeking to understand the limits of justice possible, in
terms of costs, or evils, of seeking excessive
precision at all levels is one from which
ethics as a science cannot escape.

a. Distributive justice. Distributive justice or injustice may occur whenever goods or
evils are being distributed among persons or
among groups. Distribution of goods may be
exemplified by dividing a cake at a children's
party, dividing an estate as willed by a de-
ceased person, allotment of bonuses to employees at the end of a prosperous year, payment
of quarterly stock dividends, donations of aid
to needy nations, of voting on nations for membership in the United Nations Organization.
Distribution of evils may be exemplified by
dividing chores among children, work among employees, taxes among citizens, selecting persons to be drafted for military service, re-
strictions on imports from other nations, sen-
tencing persons convicted of criminal offences,
and alloting to nations shares of the costs of
supporting the United Nations Organization.

In each actual situation where goods and/or
evils are distributed, two loci of apparent
justice and injustice need to be kept in mind.
Distribution involves both a distributer and
the distributees. Justice and injustice may
characterize both giving and receiving. Since
givers and receivers may have different esti-
mations of what distribution is just in a given

situation, questions occur about whether distributive justice involves two kinds of justice, that of the giver and that of the receivers, which may or may not be correlative. (De-
fendants in court cases often believe that they
have been sentenced unjustly.) Ethics as a science has another task, namely, that of helping
enlightened self-interested groups to conduct
their distributive functions in ways that will
reduce unrealistic noncorrelativity between
these two kinds of justice.

Two kinds of injustice need to be kept in
mind. If justice consists in giving or receiving a particular amount of good or evil,
then when a distributer gives some less than
that particular amount, the distributer is unjust and the receiver receives unjustly. But
injustice exists also when a distributer gives
some more than the particular amoung and a receiver receives more than the particular amount.
Injustice is invariance from justice both by
giving or receiving less than is just and by
giving or receiving more than is just. Somehow people seem to forget easily that giving or
receiving more than is just is also unjust.

Understanding the nature of justice and injustice may be aided by two terms, "equality"
and "deserving." Problems involved in understanding how distributive justice involves
equality among recipients have been explored
previously. When the recipients are also unequal in some respects what is received is often
valued differently by them. Justice requires
treating equals equally and also treating unequals unequally (equally unequally). But when
the inequalities apparent to recipients are not
apparent to the distributer, he cannot take them
into account. Again increased factual knowledge
by all may help to reduce both actual and apparent inequalities and injusticies.

Problems in understanding distributive jus-

tice may be both simplified and complexified
by employment of the term "deserving." On the
one hand, they are simplified, for justice consists in givng and receiving what is deserved.
Injustice exists when one gets less than he
deserves or more than he deserves. On the other hand, difficulties inhere in trying to decide
what persons or groups deserve. Where what is
deserved is defined by law, problems are comparatively easy. But when individual differences are taken into account regarding recipients' abilities, services, needs, efficient usage of receipts and comparative enjoyments or
sufferings, then what each person deserves is
often very unclear. Do persons in developing
countries deserve some minimum of human rights
only because they are born? Or do differences
in natures involve differences in natural
rights? Can a person have rights to what he
does not deserve? Despite the difficulties
raised by these questions and other questions
about the nature of deserving, ethics as a
science can hardly escape dealing with them.
It will need help from many other sciences.

b. Retributive justice. Retributive justice is both like and different from distributive justice.

(1) Differences. Distributive justice involves at least one giver and two or more receivers, whether persons or groups. Retributive justice involves at least two persons or
groups acting both as givers and receivers,
and as givers and receivers to each other.
To retribute is to give or pay back. Retributive justice involves a receiver giving back
to the giver justly (equally), or as much as
deserved, or as much as agreed upon, or as much
as is just under whatever method of deciding
is appropriate; the giver thereby becomes a
receiver.

(2) Similarities. In addition to those

mentioned at the beginning of Section 6, retributive justice also involves problems of
inequalities of givers and gifts and of receivers and of receipts, of treating equals
equally and unequals unequally (equally unequally), of differences in deservingness, of
injustice existing both when a giver gives
less than he receives or more than he receives
and when a receiver receives less that he gives
or more than he gives, and differing natures
and abilities of different persons and groups.

Retributive justice and injustice occur not
merely between two persons or two peer groups,
but also between members and their group, and
between groups and higher-level groups of
which they are members. It occurs between
groups higher up and lower down in hierarchies
of groups. It occurs between groups of different kinds, i.e., between different special
purpose groups and between general purpose and
special purpose groups. The more kinds of
groups that exist and the more complexly interdependent groups become, the more intricate
do problems of justice and injustice become.

(3) Reciprocity. Retributive justice involves the principle of reciprocity. According to the principle of reciprocity, people
tend to treat each other as they are treated
by others. Retributive justice is a natural
characteristic of the operation of this principle. Or, more accurately, retributive justice and injustice are natural characteristics
of the operation of the principle of reciprocity because it does not operate with mathematical precision.

Another task of ethics as a science, in addition to that mentioned earlier about achieving reliable generalizations about the varieties of ways that the principle of reciprocity
operates between different persons, is that of
achieving reliable generalizations about the

varieties of ways in which it operates between groups of different kinds under varying
circumstances. Also, to what extent do the
principle of reciprocity and practices regarding retributive justice and injustice, which
appear to me to be quite interdependent, actually involve each other. If significant differences are found, then the task becomes one
of generalizing about these differences also.
As evidence accumulates, enough to warrant
generalizations about workings of the principle of reciprocity, persons especially concerned with problems pertaining to retributive
justice should be able to appeal to them as
factual data providing additional enlightenment relevant to solving their problems.

Life, even merely family life, is sufficiently complicated so that repayment often
cannot be made in kind but also that some
kinds of repayment must be made to still other
persons. Husband and wife behave reciprocally
and retributively even if somewhat unequally.
But father and son, as Confucius observed in
ancient times, have much greater difficulty
in treating each other equally. The father
supports his son, but the son cannot support
his father. An expert in the doctrine of
treating unequals as equally unequal ("dis-
criminating love"), Confucius formulated a
rule, based on the principle of reciprocity
as a more complex principle (a principle of
family life and not merely of relations between to people), as follows: Treat each
other particular person as you would like to
be treated if you were that person. A father
should treat his son as a son, and not as an
equal; but he should treat his son (equally)
as he would like to be treated if he were his
son. A son cannot repay to his father for
the support that his father has given him. But
being a family man, he can treat his own son

as his father treated him. The principle of
reciprocity operates in this way also, now
processually, from father to son who becomes a
father to a son who becomes a father to a son,
etc.

When one observes the perpetual operation of
the principle of reciprocity in human associ-
atings, present in some way and degree in every
interaction, he must become impressed with its
importance. It is not just something occurring
in occasional examples but is something perme-
ating the nature of each self, each primary
group, and, even if less obviously, of all
groups. Each person, for example, both remains
the same as giver and receiver in each social
interaction. But also, to the extent that what
he receives back as a gift from his companion
involves some element (e.g., an idea) that is
new to him which he then incorporates into his
own being, he becomes that much different. When
he then reciprocates his own new gift to the
other, and the other receives and incorporates
it into his self, he also remains the same self
and becomes somewhat different. When the other
then responds, as a self that is both the same
and also different because a newly added element
in creatively responding, our first person then
receives not only a gift from the other but a
gift embodying effects of the first giver's gift
in such a way that when he embodies the other's
gift within himself, he is reembodying a part of
himself as given through his gift to the other.

This process, properly called dialectic, is
a natural example of how the principle of reciprocity works processually in human association,
reciprocally increasing values in each of the
associated. Understanding how the principle of
reciprocity works dialectically is another task
for ethics as a science, even if it is one that
most contemporary ethicists seem unprepared to
try to understand. Understanding dialectical

perpetuation of reembodiments of the principle of reciprocity in processual association
should prove useful for understanding problems,
theoretical and practical, of retributive and
distributive justice and injustice. It should
be most useful in increasing enlightenment regarding the natures of both persons and groups
needed by those who would pursue self-interest
wisely.

7. Wise self-interest. The self-interestedness of groups is inseparable from the self-
interestedness of persons, and the enlightenment and wisdom manifest in group decisions
does not exceed that of the members and officers actively engaged in formulating group
policies. But members and officers responsible for group policies do tend both to pursue
the best interests of the group as a group
(i.e., all of its interests) and to achieve
as much enlightenment as conveniently possible and to choose as wisely as such enlightenment indicates.

Wisely self-interested groups adopt policies regarding services to members and especially to officers (all employees) that will encourage such persons to choose and act as members in ways that are best for the group as a
group without unjustly favoring themselves
merely as persons. Pursuit of enlightenment
and wisdom is more important for groups than
for persons to the extent that the well being
of many persons is at stake in group decisions
when the well being of only one person is at
stake in merely personal decisions. However,
when, and to the extent that, the welfare of
a group depends primarily on decisions by one
person as a responsible officer, then enlightenment and wisdom in that person is more important than in a group when and because it
functions as enlightenment and wisdom for the
group in crucial decisions.

Kinds of actions that wisely self-interested groups ought to enact include the following:

a. Increase enlightenment. Groups can do
what they most ought to do, or what is right
for them to do, better if they more clearly and
more fully understand their natures and purposes
and how best to pursue and fulfill those purposes.
Thus each group ought to increase its enlightenment about its nature and purposes and methods
as much as possible, other things being equal.
Usually assistance from several sciences will
be needed. When and because groups can improve
their self-understanding by aid from other sciences, they have vested interests in supporting
and promoting those sciences. Enlightenment
remains incomplete until understanding of the
basic presuppositions involved in explaining
their natures, purposes, methods, and the other
sciences on which they depend, has been obtained. Hence enlightenment should include understanding of the basic philosophical (metaphysical, epistemological, axiological, ethical,
logical, etc.) presuppositions inherent in such
explanations.

b. Maintain comprehension. Wise self-interestedness includes attainment and maintenance
of a comprehensive perspective of all interests
or at least of all kinds of interests. To neglect some, especially some that are important,
is to do less than what is best.

(1) These interests usually include interests
of a group (a) in itself as a group, (b) in its
members, (c) in its members as persons, (d) in
its officers and employees, (e) in its peer
groups, both cooperative and competitive, (f)
in higher-level groups, at all levels, in which
it participates, and (g) in other persons, both
as potential members, as potential enemies, and
as persons.

(2) These interests often include economic,
political, educational, recreational and reli-

gious interests generally, and accounting, banking, credit, medical, security, advancement, retirement, employee-training, customer-service, public relations, personnel, and insurance interests, for example, specifically. The more complex a group and the more comprehensive its perspective, the more it has interests in numerous specialists, both in the sciences and in the technologies.

(3) These interests usually include some awareness of the interdependence not merely of its own numerous kinds of interests but also of its interedependence with other groups. To the extent that interdependence of groups, locally, nationally, globally, continues to increase, enlightenment about the contributions that other groups are making and can make, both beneficially and harmfully, to a group's welfare becomes a more important issue. When its benefits from other groups depend partly on its own benefits to those other groups, wise self-interest includes attention to those benefits.

c. Balance functions. In addition to keeping all kinds of interests in mind, each group has an interest in devoting its efforts to all such interests in ways appropriate to their natures and optimal contributions to its welfare. Overemphasis on one or some at the expense of others usually results in what is less than the best. Neglect or underemphasis of one or some usually results in what is less than the best. Imbalance is a kind of reductionism. Extreme reductionism takes one interest, a part of the whole or all of a group's interests, and subordinates all other interests to it. Less extreme imbalances may result in less deficiency, but trying to maintain the best balance among a group's interests is itself a kind of interest important for wise self-interest.

d. Exploit beneficial means. To the extent that principles of reciprocity have been
demonstrated to work in various ways with some
degrees of reliability in intergroup behavior,
each group should seek enlightenment regarding
them and then utilize them when benefits promise to be greater than costs. In addition to
supporting and utilizing information from numerous sciences, awareness of its need for ex-
ploiting the benefits from interdisciplinary
research institutes and thus for supporting and
utilizing information from them should constitute another interest of growing importance to
wisely self-interested groups.

e. Reduce harmful conflicts. Enlightened
groups normally are aware of some conflicts of
interests both within and between groups. Wisely self-interested groups will try to eliminate or reduce those conflcts that appear harmful.

f. Sustain morale. Not only should groups
seek what is best for their members, including
officers, but part of what is best for them is
to be aware, at least occasionally and as con-
tinuously as possible, that it is in fact doing
its best to seek what is best for them. Awareness of achievement of success in such efforts
tends to contribute to morale. And morale is
itself a great value, both as a useful asset
and as intrinsic value existing in the enjoyments of its members. Hence groups should seek
to escape from the evils of bureaucracy. Groups
should make it unprofitable to officers to pursue their self-interests as persons at the expense of the group. Wisely self-interested
groups will make it unprofitable to members to
violate its regulations involving the rights
and duties of the group and of its members.

g. Attend to adaptability. Most groups confront both needs for stability and needs for
adaptability. Wisely self-interested groups

will give sufficient attention to both kinds
of needs. Adaptation to small changes and to
changes with short-range effects often occurs
without requiring additional enlightenment.
But larger, more complex, more profound changes
often require much greater enlightenment. This
problem confronting groups as groups is interinvolved with each group's culture. Group
wise self-interestedness includes understanding of, sensitivity to, and successful efforts
to overcome, the evils of cultural lag.

CULTURE

1. Nature of culture. Culture consists in
commonly-participated-in behavior patterns that
are not innate but acquired after birth by
learning. Except for ideas, attitudes or practices that are newly invented, ideas, attitudes
and practices patterning common behavior are
acquired from others. All culture is by nature
something transmittable from person to person,
often from generation to generation for centuries.
2. Kinds of culture. Culture includes language, folkways, mores and institutions, including ideas about the best ways of saying and
doing things, both in dealing with plants and
animals and other natural resources and in dealing with other persons. Some kinds of culture
develop merely as a result of habit, exemplified
by a path going around one side of a tree instead of the other side because the first person walking that way happened to go around the
one side. Some kinds of culture are establish-
by ruler's fiat. Some kinds are established
by group decision. As societies become more
complex, specialists in legislation are em-
powered to determine much of our culture at
least as guides to the kinds of behavior desired by groups.

Culture includes ideas and ideals about how people ought to behave in some kinds of situations, and often includes mandatory kinds of behavior at critical stages in life, such as birth, adolescence, marriage, induction into an occupation, divorce and death. It usually includes ideas about the best ways of behaving relative to each major kind of group function: economic, political, educational, religious, medical, martial, etc. The relative compulsiveness with which conformity of persons to the ideas established in a group's consensus has been exemplified by distinguishing between folkways (unenforced common patterns), mores (opinion-enforced common patterns), and institutions (authority-enforced common patterns). Institutions, in this sense, include laws with penalties, and the vast police, judicial and penal systems is designed to enforce behavior patterns believed to be, if not essential to group welfare, at least best for group welfare.

A person not conforming to folkways may be judged queeer, but not immoral. But violations of the mores and institutions are regarded as immoral or unethical. Although neither their conditional nature nor the reasons why the compulsory behavior patterns are considered good are always clear to those who learn about them. Too often mores and institutions are taught and learned as absolute, and penalties assessed for violations reenforce such learning. When this occurs, too many persons misunderstand ethical codes and principles as absolute, i.e., as without exception and unchangeable, and as objective or real, i.e., as something preexisting persons and as something to which persons must conform.

3. Cultural lag. Cultural lag occurs whenever institutions intended to serve needs of a group no longer do so. The most enlightening account of the nature of cultural lag that I have found centers about what is called "The

Cycle of Institutional Development."[3] Although
the cycle is more or less continuous, five or
six stages can be distinguished.

a. Initiation. When a self-interested group
discovers that some of its needs are not being
met through institutionalized cooperation, suggestions occur regarding what institutional
forms, or behavior patterns, will best fill the
needs. When one of these suggestions is adopted and tried out, then its institutionalization
begins.

b. Efficiency. When the new institution
does serve the group's needs most beneficially,
the stage is described as one of efficiency.
Persons who participate in the institution
find that it serves their needs, so they naturally not only approve its existence but also
support it as a good means to their own ends.
Persons and institutions now complement each
other. People not only do what they ought to
do in conforming or participating, but they do
so willingly as a beneficial means to their
own ends. Institutions as conditional oughts
participate in actual oughts automatically because persons seeking to do what is best for
themselves participate in them unhesitatingly.

c. Formalism. Unfortunately for social and
cultural felicity, changes occur in groups in
ways that both call for new institutions to
meet newer needs and result in older institutions becoming less useful because the older
needs have declined in importance. When institutions established in a group to compel
conformity no longer serve the needs of members efficiently, especially when they no
longer serve any needs of some members, people
feel compelled to conform to them without
benefitting from such conformity. Persons
feeling compelled to participate in the institutions feel that they must serve the institutions without being served by them. The forms

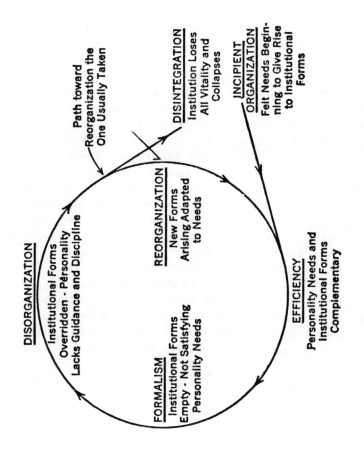

are empty of value, and gradually acquire a
negative value, as the costs of conformity
increasingly outweigh the former benefits.

d. Disorganization. When institutional
forms compel service but do not serve, new
members of the group cannot understand why
conformity should continue. Unless penalties
of nonconformity are too great, they refuse to
conform. Conformity, for them is unethical.
In choosing and doing what is best for themselves, they believe that they ought not to
conform, i.e., to pay costs for no benefits.
When some members of a group do and some do
not conform, the institution is in a stage
of disorganization. Those who do conform regard those who do not as immoral. Those who
do not conform regard those who do conform as
foolish. Lack of agreement regarding the values of conformity tends to cripple cooperation
regarding the institution and lack of organization itself is often an evil infecting loyal-
ties to other institutions of the group.

e. Disintegration. When fewer and fewer
members of a group participate and conform,
an institution weakens and deteriorates. Especially when the needs that it was designed
to serve have disappeared, or have diminished
in importance, institutions naturally disinte-
grate sooner or later.

f. Reorganization. If the needs served by
the institution persist, then newer institutional forms tend to be suggested. Reformed
institutions rather than no institutions are
called for. Designing new forms to serve the
needs most fittingly is often difficult, since
older minds recall benefits of the older ways
and newer minds lack experience needed for
demonstrating reliability of proposed new ways.
Delayed reform often begets revolutionary reforms. When reforms are adopted too soon,
evolutionary reforms retain more elements of

cultural lag.

Although institutions are ethical in the
sense that they are intended to serve as means
whereby groups can increase the best results
for the group (including its members) through
cooperative action needed to attain such results, awareness that cultural lag prevents institutions from serving as intended creates an
awareness that the institution ought to be
changed. Thus members both ought to participate
in a group's institutions, when and because they
are intended to produce the best results for
them as members, and ought not to participate
in them, when and because they nc longer serve
as intended. The more institutions are infect-
ed by cultural lag, the more members ought to
try to have them disappear or be reformed. Persons introduced to institutions during their
stages of formalism and disorganization can be
expected to be, i.e., they ought to be, anti-
institutional. Such persons often do not understand the institutions because they are not
acquainted with their initiating purposes and
their obvious benefits during the stage of efficiency.

4. Social intelligence. A wisely self-interested society keeps its institutions at the
stage of efficiency as much as possible. And,
if and when formalism, disorganization and reorganization occur, it will endeavor to reduce
the time consumed by these stages. Enlightenment regarding a group's nature and needs, not
merely in the past and present but also in a
future in which changes are to be expected,
usually indicates need for social planning;
how much enlightenment is possible regarding
future uncertainties as peoples and their institutions and processes become nore intricately interdependent is itself quite uncertain.
But social scientists already know enough
about institutions and processes to be able

to make some beneficial recommendations. En-
acting laws with terminating dates automatically eliminates those laws from further cultural lag.

Action is intelligent when it attains the
benefits it seeks most efficiently, i.e., at-
taining the most good at the cost of the least
evil. Societies are intelligent when groups
perform their functions and serve their purposes through institutions that are most efficient. Ethics as a science has the task of
understanding and teaching how groups can keep
their institutions at the stage of efficiency
as much as possible. Ethics as a science has
the task of showing wisely self-interested
groups how to improve their social intelligence.

NOTES

NOTES

Chapter I. THE IMPORTANCE OF ETHICS

Omitted.

Chapter II. THE NATURE OF OUGHTNESS

1. "Evil" and "bad" are synonyms for present

purposes.

2. This statement is intended as an hypothesis, in the sense described in Chapter II, "The Nature of Science," in <u>Axiology: The Science of Values</u>. Stating hypotheses here as facts facilitates understanding needed for developing more complicated hypotheses later. Retention of an attitude of tentativity regarding all scientific conclusions is intended here and in all of the assertions made in the following.

3. Whether, and to what extent, subconscious and unconscious factors enter into choices is not examined here. If research reveals such factors as present and as significant in some choices, this hypothesis will need appropriate modification. I refer here not to subconscious and unconscious factors in-influencing appearances, which are to be expected, but to subconscious and unconscious factors causing a choice between an apparently greater good and an apparently lesser good to be different from the norm stated in the above descriptions.

4. This problem of uncertainty about appearances confronts each scientist each time he makes a choice relative to an issue arising in his project. He must make a choice on the basis of what appears to him. To the extent that he retains awareness of the need for keeping an attitude of tentativity regarding his conclusions, this is a factor in what appears to him. His choice, like all other choices, is an ethical one, even though he may not be aware of it as such.

5. I have not discussed the causal conditions of experience, awareness, appearance, feelings, enjoyments, sufferings, awareness of differences, comparisons, and of accepting and asserting about all of them. This is another set of scientific problems. I trust that the

physiological psychologists working on them are making progress. Any compulsiveness contributed by such causes and conditions is an additional kind of force not examined here.

6. Any scientists having doubts about the nature of the compellingness of choosing be-between apparently greater and lesser values should consider whether or not he has any doubts about the compellingness of his choosing to assert that five is a larger number than four when the two numbers appear for comparison. If he is able to give an account that satisfied him about the nature of such feeling of compulsion relative to numbers, then I suggest that he use the same explanation to account for the feelings of compulsion relative to choosing between apparently greater and lesser values. If he believes that comparing numbers and comparing values are different, then let him ask himself, "Ought I not assert that five is a larger number than four?" One does not escape oughtness in dealing with numbers. The apparent largerness of five when compared with four is obvious; so one ought to say that it is. Working a mathematical problem involves a person in a series of inferences each of which involves a choice, and each choice involves oughtness. Every mathematical problem is an ethical problem or, rather, a series of ethical problems. When a mathematician does what he ought to do, then he usually gets the "right" answer.

7. See Axiology: The Science of Ethics, Ch. III.

8. The following list is adapted from my Ethics as a Behavioral Science, pp. 136-142. Charles C Thomas, Springfield, Ill., 1974.

9. See Section 2, below.

10. See "Knowledge of Values," Ch. IV, in Axiology: The Science of Values. See also

Ethics as a Behavioral Science, Ch. IV.

11. See further, Ethics as a Behavioral Science, pp. 142-149. See also my Metaphysics: An Introduction, Ch. 32. Barnes and Noble, N.Y., 1974.

12. When a person faced with two alternatives that appear to be exactly equal chooses not to choose between them, he actually chooses between two other alternatives, i.e., between choosing and not choosing between them.

13. See Archie J. Bahm, "Freedom is Fitness," The Scientific Monthly, Vol. LXIII, No. 4, August, 1946, pp. 135-136. For a more extended treatment, see my Philosophy: An Introduction, pp. 321-327. John Wiley and Sons, N.Y., 1953.

14. Persons holding materialistic, spiritualistic or dualistic metaphysical views may be aided by reading Chapters 18, 19 and 20, especially pp. 245-248, of my Philosophy: An Introduction, or my Metaphysics: An Introduction, Chs. 19-33, especially pp. 168-174.

15. Many sects and doctrines have done so. But unless investigation by scientific ethicists confirms the conditional bestness of their limitations, I believe that they should be included in such developments.

16. See Archie J. Bahm, "Theories of Conscience," Ethics, Vol. LXXV, No. 2, January, 1965, pp. 128-131.

17. My hypothesis about conscience is essentially negative, even if only mildly so, and is held much more tentatively than my hypothesis about the nature of oughtness. Many persons learning about ethics in terms of "Stop!" "Don't!" "No! No!" regard ethics as essentially negative. I trust that I have corrected this view so far as ethics as a science is concerned. That is, although ethics depends on two values, good and bad, more or less equally, and on appeals to choose the

greater of two goods as well as the lesser
of two evils, ethics will be understood better and learned more easily and practiced
more approvingly if it is presented as positive primarily or as positive and negative
equally than if it is presented as negative
primarily. Since my hypothesis about the
nature of conscience, as fear that one will
not choose, or otherwise achieve, the greatest good, is essentially negative, I welcome
further research inquiring whether conscience
may be equally positive, e.g., as enjoyment
of confidence experienced when working "con-
scientiously."

18. Exodus, 20:12.
19. See my Metaphysics: An Introduction, Chs.
    8, 11, 12, 13, 19-33.
20. See further, "Ways in Which All Ethical Sit-
    uations Are Alike," Ch. 2, in Ethics as a
    Behavioral Science.
21. See Archie J. Bahm, The Specialist, especi-
    ally Part I. The Macmillan Company of India,
    New Delhi; World Books, Albuquerque, 1977.
22. These principles, developed more fully in my
    Why Be Moral? An Introduction to Ethics, were
    first published in Philosophy Today, Vol. 9,
    Spring, 1965, pp. 52-60.
23. The nature of values, intrinsic and instru-
    mental, is explained in Axiology: The Science
    of Values, Ch. III.
24. I willingly spare readers unnecessary lin-
    guistic jargon: "metaoughtness," and "actual
    and conditional metaoughtness," etc.
25. Archie J. Bahm, "Rightness Defined," Phi-
    losophy and Phenomenological Research, Vol.
    8, No. 2, December, 1947, pp. 266-268.
26. Although I have refrained from discussing
    dialectic in the present volume, I believe
    that progress in scientific research gener-
    ally will discover dialectic, a word tabooed
    except as associated with Hegelian and Marx-

ian philosophies, as an omnipresent characteristic of all processes and will adopt
a metaphysics, epistemology, logic, and
philosophy of scientific method recognizing
and utilizing dialectical concepts more ade-
quately revealing the nature of such processes. E.g., see my Metaphysics: An Introduction, pp. 207-230, and my Polarity, Dialectic, and Organicity, Charles C Thomas, Springfield, Ill., 1970.

Chapter III. PERSONAL ETHICS

1. The current chaos, dominated by several special-interest groups in psychology (like the
chaos in philosophy and several other sciences), is detrimental not only to psychology
but also to ethics, the social sciences, and
all others that depend on it. I believe that
it is in the national interest to have more
intelligent guidance for research in psychology, just as I do in axiology and ethics.
2. See my "Organicism: The Philosophy of Interdependence," International Philosophical
Quarterly, Vol. VII, No. 2, June, 1967, pp.
251-284. See also my The Philosopher's
World Model, Ch. IV, Greenwood Press, West-
port, Conn., 1979.
3. See his Mind, Self, and Society, University
of Chicago Press, Chicago, 1934.
4. L. L. Bernard, Introduction to Social Psychology, p. 343. Henry Holt and Co., N.Y.,1926.
5. Ethics as a science depends on the conclusions of social psychologists regarding kinds
and norms of development of self-interests,
e.g., including genetic psychology, infant
psychology, child psychology, adolescent
psychology, adult psychology, and the psychology of aging.
6. Charles Horton Cooley, R. C. Angell, and L.
J. Carr, Introductory Sociology, p. 55.

244

Charles Scribner's Sons, N.Y., 1933.

7. Ibid.

8. See ibid., pp. 58-68.

9. See my "Is American Society Ethically Deficient?" Journal of Social Philosophy, Vol. V., No. 3, Sept., 1974, pp. 8-9.

10. E.g., see criticisms of the dualistic philosophy of Rene' Descartes in my Philosophy: An Introduction, Ch. 13.

11. For exploration of problems regarding whole-part complementarity, including complementarity of temporal wholes and parts and whole-part causation, see my Metaphysics: An Introduction, Chs. 10, 11, 24.

12. A fourfold classification of interests that I have found enlightening and useful is one originated by W. I. Thomas and Florian Znaneiki in The Polish Peasant in Europe and America, Vol. I, p. 73, A. A. Knopf, N.Y., 1918, 1927, and developed by Joseph K. Folsom, Social Psychology, Ch. IV, Harper and Brothers, N.Y., 1931.

13. See my Philosophy of the Buddha, Harper and Brothers, N.Y., 1962.

14. See my The World's Living Religions, pp. 206-222. Dell Publishing Co., N.Y., 1964; Southern Illinois University Press, Carbondale, 1971; Arnold-Heinemann, New Delhi, 1977.

15. See my The Specialist, Part III. Macmillan Company of India, New Delhi, 1977; World Books, Albuquerque, 1977.

16. For further examination of these ten principles, see my Why Be Moral? An Introduc- to Ethics, Ch. V. Munshiram Manoharlal Publisher, New Delhi, 1980.

17. For an earlier study, see Why Be Moral? Ch. IX.

18. See The World's Living Religions, especially Chapter I.

Chapter IV. SOCIAL ETHICS

1. Ethics as a science has a duty, in conjuntion with sociology and psychology, to discover what, if any, principles for choosing (conditional oughts) inhere in the natures of each of these kinds of group self-inter est. I have already proposed several principles for choosing pertaining to a group and its members, in <u>Why Be Moral? An Introduction to Ethics</u>, pp. 335ff. Munshiram Manoharlal Publisher, New Delhi, 1980.

2. The word "officers" as used here includes all engaged in serving the group, for wages or otherwise, i.e., in the most menial tasks as well as those of administration.

3. See Charles Horton Cooley, Robert Cooley Angell and Lowell J. Carr, <u>Introductory Sociology</u>, pp. 406-415. Charles Scribner's Sons, N.Y., 1933. The chart is from p. 496.

Chapter V. OTHER ETHICAL SCIENCES

Omitted.

DATE DUE